# Death on a Dark Highway

The Murder of Dennis Brooks, Jr.

By Jim Chandler

ISBN 1452834512

EAN-13 is 9781452834511

Printed in the United States of America

It was hot in the Tennessee countryside on the evening of Thursday July 29, 1993. Even approaching midnight the residual heat blanketed the rolling plains of northwestern Tennessee in Carroll County, a 600-square mile dot of small towns and rural farms, known best perhaps as the birthplace of the late actress Dixie Carter and country singer Jessica Andrews.

Things were about to get hotter. Before the sun broke the morning horizon, the area would awaken to the most horrific murder in the memory of even the old-timers. A promising young life would be snuffed out in a manner sufficiently grisly to turn the stomach of even the stoutest soul. And three local young people, one an attractive young woman, would eventually pay the price for the dirty deed, albeit in the eyes of most a price not nearly high enough.

On Highway 114, between the small communities of Buena Vista and Hollow Rock, Keith Noles and his wife fought the heat by sleeping on their enclosed front porch with all the windows open.

Awakened between 12:30 and 1:00 a.m. by voices coming from the road about a hundred feet away, Keith could see the taillights of a vehicle through a thicket of sapling trees and could hear bits and pieces of conversation. At one point, he heard someone say something about "ten dollars," and then a male voice yelling, *I've got it covered, I've got it covered!* Moments later a male voice cried, *If you move the truck I'll blow your goddamn head off, do you hear me?* Noles heard a voice that sounded female yell, *Lay down, motherfucker, lay down!*

He shook his wife, Jonnie, who was still asleep. "I think somebody is fixing to be shot," he told her. Moments after Jonnie awoke, there was an explosion followed by a high, keening scream. Jonnie thought the cry that tore through the darkness came from a woman. Both listeners then heard a female scream, *Lay down*, after which the truck sped away in the direction of Hollow Rock, the taillights disappearing from sight through the foliage.

Keith Noles hurriedly dressed and rushed down to the spot where the vehicle had been parked, searching for some clue as to what had happened. There, he found a wet spot on the macadam that looked suspiciously like blood. He returned to his house and phoned the Carroll County Sheriff's Department in Huntingdon, reporting what he and his wife had seen and heard.

Thus began the opening chapter of what was to become one of the most gruesome events ever to unfold in Carroll County history. It would resonate in an area where residents seldom failed to stop and offer help to anyone along the roadways, no matter the time of day or night.

That was all about to change in a big way.

Later on Friday, Dennis Brooks, Sr. became somewhat concerned when his son did not show up at his home around noon as planned. His son, Dennis Jr., had found a pickup truck he wanted to buy and had asked his dad to accompany him to look at the vehicle, since his father was more knowledgeable about what was or was not a good deal. He owned a 1984 Ford Ranger but, like most young people his age, wanted to trade up to something a little newer. Dennis had seen his son the evening before when they all had dinner with his wife's mother, and there had been no mention of a change of plan.

Brooks Sr., who owned and operated a landscaping business, had moved his family to Carroll County from Memphis about a dozen years earlier. He would later say that he had done so to escape the crime so prevalent in the urban setting of the Bluff City—a statement that displays how horrifically irony sometimes affects the human condition.

Young Dennis, a 1992 graduate of Clarksburg High School, was a student at Jackson State Community College majoring in criminal justice, set to enter his sophomore year in the fall. He also worked at the Subway Restaurant in Huntingdon. He was perhaps a poster boy for how one would wish a son to be—a good, decent kid with a focus on the future and an understanding of the place he would occupy in it.

The young man closed the Subway alone that fateful night sometime between 12:30 and 1:00 a.m. Never in his wildest imagination could he have conceived of what awaited him on Highway 114 as he made his way to a house owned by his grandfather, who lived in Memphis and stayed there infrequently. Like most people in the area, a part of the country famous for its hospitality and friendly ways, he would not think twice about stopping to aid a woman stranded along the dark rural highway. He would never have dreamed in his worst nightmare that two armed men hid in the darkness behind the broken truck and that they planned to hijack—and likely kill—the first random motorist who stopped.

His decency in this case was his undoing. One can only imagine the terror he must have felt when he stopped in response to the young blonde woman's frantic signals, only to be confronted by two screaming thugs rushing at him out of the darkness, one armed with a 20-gauge shotgun. There were curses and screams as he was thrown to the road and then ordered into the bed of the pickup, according to the pair of witnesses who lived very near where the truck was stopped. Then, there was a loud report as the shotgun fired, followed by a high keening wail; an accidental shot, according to later testimony by the man who pulled the trigger. Young Brooks had received a terrible wound to the hip and lower abdominal area, an injury that would have, the state medical examiner later said, proven mortal, as well as excruciatingly painful. And then, fleeing high-speed in the hijacked truck toward Hollow Rock, Smothers administered the *coup de grace* to the victim as he pleaded to be taken to the hospital.

That final shot, fired with the shotgun barrel pressed under Dennis Brooks' chin, silenced his cries forevermore.

When Dennis did not show up at his father's house shortly after noon July 30 and could not be located, the elder Brooks became concerned. It was not like his son to miss an appointment without notifying him. So, after driving out to the farm to see if he could find his son and a check of several of his friends turned up no clue as to where he might be, Dennis Sr. called the Carroll County Sheriff's Office and reported him missing. Road deputies were advised to be on the lookout for the young man's truck and helicopters from the Tennessee Highway Patrol and the Henry County Sheriff's Office took to the sky for a look. As in most rural areas, there were dense woodlands along the road where a vehicle might crash and not be visible to passing motorists, one of the fears that surely engaged the mind of the missing man's father that afternoon. Injured, and dead, motorists have been known to lie in wrecked cars for days before being discovered under such circumstances.

Late Friday afternoon, a helicopter crew spotted a pickup truck smoldering in a field just off Langford Store Road in the northeastern part of the county. A county fire unit was dispatched, along with several deputies, and a grisly discovery was made once the fire was extinguished. Inside the cab were the burned and dismembered remains of a human being. The missing young man had been found, dental charts would prove once the remains were transported to Memphis.

Before the weekend was over, a murderous trio of young county residents would be taken into custody and charged with homicide and kidnapping. Finding them was not that difficult, because they had left a trail of evidence a mile long: a broken pickup belonging to one of them very near the reported scene of an altercation and shooting; a burned pickup and victim within about a mile of where all three lived close together on Dillahunty Road; and lastly, two of them were found to be wearing clothing, a cap and new Nike sneakers, taken from the dead man. The young man wearing the sneakers, a fellow later said to have an IQ of 81 according to a psychologist, had not even bothered to wipe the victim's blood off the shoes.

The Tennessee Bureau of Investigation came into the case immediately after discovery of the homicide, which is standard operating procedure in Carroll County. The TBI has the reputation as an organization with capable investigators and the kinds of forensic equipment necessary to work a serious case to a successful conclusion.

TBI Special Agent Alvin Daniels of Camden took over as the lead investigator. Unfortunately, Daniels would suffer from terminal cancer all during the legal proceedings and succumb to the disease shortly after the entire case played out. So ill was Daniels that his preliminary court testimony was preserved, over objections of the defense, to have it on record in the event he did not live to testify at the upcoming trials. It was Daniels, assisted by CCSO Investigator David Bunn, who questioned the three persons charged with Brooks' murder, gaining admissions from each of them.

Arrested the day after the murder were Walter S. Smothers, Teresa Deion Harris and Stacy Ramsey, all of the Huntingdon area. Smothers, 25, had a record of some misdemeanor offenses, including DUI and vandalism of a cemetery, but there was nothing in his background to suggest he might perpetrate something as chilling as the Brooks murder. Harris, 22, a petite and attractive blonde woman who lived with Smothers at her Dillahunty Road residence, certainly had nothing in her past to indicate that she was a potential killer, although she had a history

7

of drug and alcohol use from an early age and had allegedly been the victim of sexual abuse.

Ramsey, 22, a relative newcomer to the area who lived across the road from Smothers and Harris, seemed to be an unlikely killer as well. The lanky young man was regarded as a good worker by his employer and was well liked by everyone who knew him. His truck and shotgun were used in the murder, but he did not know Smothers until the day of the killing. They met after Harris sent her young son across the road to invite him to come and "smoke a joint" with them, and then followed up later with an invitation herself when Ramsey did not immediately come over.

Later testimony would prove that the trio, high on an array of alcohol and drugs, set out that evening to locate David Hampton, an ex-boyfriend of Harris, a man perhaps saved by the fact that Ramsey's truck locked up before they could find him. It seems that Harris was incensed over a leather jacket she had placed in lay-away for him while they were dating. It appeared to be an unlikely reason to commit murder, even if she had paid much of the cost and he had sprung only for the last few bucks to retrieve it. However, there were also the phone calls the former lover continued to make to her, the last of which was intercepted by Smothers the evening of the murder. The two men had argued and decided to punch it out, though there was some doubt about when the fisticuffs were to take place. In any case, it led to the trip that culminated in the horrific and senseless slaughter of Dennis Brooks, Jr.

The public got its first glimpse of the killers on Monday following the Friday morning murder, when the trio faced arraignment in Carroll County General Sessions Court. Normally an insecure facility with no metal detectors or permanent security staff in place, the courthouse became a virtual bastion as authorities worried over the possibility of reprisals against the group, so high ran feelings in the community. Practically every police officer in the county flooded into and around the building, several on the upper floors armed with hand-held metal detectors. The officers frisked everyone and took pocketknives and other sharp implements—even from members of the media who had known the deputies for years.

There were two courtrooms on the second floor of the ornate granite structure. The larger was used during general sessions proceedings and also during circuit jury trials. It would hold about three hundred people and perhaps a few more if packed in the standing area.

The smaller room across the hall was set aside primarily for chancery court. Getting forty people inside it would be a chore. In order to maintain security and to keep down the number of spectators in attendance, the small room was chosen for the arraignment that Monday. Officers allowed entry only to members of the victim's family, media and court officials and the doors were locked and heavily guarded. Cardboard inserts blocked the two small glass panes in the hallway doors to keep down the distraction of people in the hallway peering into the room.

The last time security had posed as serious an issue in the memory of most was during a 1986 murder trial. Feelings in the community also peaked then, because an 18-year-old black man was on trial for murdering a 14-year-old white youth.

The allegation was, and evidence substantiated, that the two had been engaged in a homosexual affair and that the younger boy died from a beating with a wooden board after the defendant became fearful the victim might tell on him. A Huntingdon police officer, attracted by an overpowering stench, discovered the boy's maggot-riddled corpse under a pile of leaves three days later near the town cemetery, very near where the murder had occurred.

General Sessions Judge Larry Logan had arraigned David Houssel in that case. He was also set to arraign Smothers, Harris and Ramsey for their alleged heinous actions.

The judge had his fans and he had his detractors, but they could all agree on one thing: Logan was pretty much a 'cool cat' any way you cut it. A snappy dresser who wore his wavy hair long and looked probably a decade younger than his true mid-forties, he had a style and wit that made him something of a legend in the area—especially for his repartee with defendants. Usually a man of good cheer and impeccable fairness, the judge *could* get down and dirty when necessary, but his general tendency was to be as nice and accommodating as the defendant, and the circumstances, allowed.

Once, a man charged with entering the McKenzie City Hall with a can of gasoline and a lighter and threatening to "blow the place up" was before the judge on attempted arson charges. The defendant was what Logan joking referred to as one of his "frequent flyers"—people who appeared repeatedly in his court, generally on very piddling charges.

When Logan asked the man how he pled, the defendant replied in all seriousness, "Can't you just give me the death penalty, Your Honor?"

"Well, you're not charged with a capital offense," the judge replied, smiling. "But I'm sure most of these officers would be happy to take you out behind the courthouse and shoot you." Several of the police officers nodded in agreement with that possibility, most trying to suppress a laugh.

On the other hand, Logan had once sentenced four parents whose kids had repeatedly skipped school to serve ten days in jail, after finding them guilty of abetting truancy. He was a judge who had his priorities well defined and if he saw humor where it existed, he likewise understood that sometimes punishment was the only solution.

The trio came in before a thoroughly humorless judge this day. All sported "belly chains," a device to which their hands were cuffed to a chain encircling their waists, and all wore ankle shackles. In addition, Smothers and Ramsey's chains were attached rather closely, effectively negating any thoughts of escape.

Quiet sobs came from the victim's family seated on the second bench back, especially his mother, Linda. His father, Dennis, a large and powerful looking man, seemed stunned and dazed, yet his eyes bespoke something else. It did not take a mystic to understand what must be going through his mind as he gained first sight of the three who had murdered and mutilated his son two days before. If looks could have killed, the trio would have vanished into a pile of smoking cinders in an instant.

The three defendants sat in wooden chairs behind the defendant's table, Smothers behind the others. He seemed to be in the throes of a seizure, his body and limbs jerking so much that the chains binding him rattled like the soundtrack of an old ghost movie. One might have perceived that as fear, but according to the authorities it was merely the effects of withdrawal from the drugs and alcohol in his system when taken into custody; it was so bad that he had been transported to the hospital where he was given something for his nerves.

After all, the trio had indulged in beer, marijuana, Valiums and tequila on the day of the murder and had apparently continued with the chemicals afterward. Smothers and Harris were seen partying in a local tavern the night after the murder—something made even more heartless by the fact that she was wearing what turned out to be the victim's Memphis Tigers ball cap.

Of the three, Smothers was the one who would have more aptly fit Logan's "frequent flyer" designation, having appeared in court several times on charges a lot less serious than what he now faced. In fact, he had appeared for arraignment in Logan's court two days before the murder on a charge of driving on a suspended license, second offense, a charge that was still outstanding. During an August 1991 appearance, he pled guilty to charges of vandalism and leaving the scene of an accident in an incident in which a tombstone was struck by a vehicle. In the minds of many, a person who would desecrate venerated objects was among the lowest of the low; however, Smothers managed to cut a deal and wound up paying only one set of court costs, with no fine or jail time for the outrageous behavior.

Teresa Deion Harris looked somewhat out of place in court, trussed up and charged with one of the more heinous crimes ever experienced locally. Petite and with long blonde hair, she was pretty in that "girl-next-door" way, but with an edge hardened by a few years of living on the slippery side of life. She had married young, had a couple of children, and divorced. Her former husband later told the writer, "give her a couple of beers and she'd (have sex with) anybody."

Harris had had some involvement with police herself in the days leading up to the murder, but as an alleged victim and not a perpetrator. The woman reported to HPD Officer Ricky Sawyers on July 15 that her ex-husband had slapped her several times after she gave him a ride to his mother's house. She declined to press charges, however.

Logan ascertained that the defendants had not retained legal counsel. In most cases, the court makes some effort to determine if defendants can afford to pay for legal representation, but the severity of the charges facing the trio made that procedure moot. The judge indicated that he would appoint representation for the three shortly and ordered that they be held without bond pending a preliminary hearing August 6.

The defendants were in and out of the courtroom in less than five minutes, for all the wall of security and extra precautions. It was the first of many court appearances to come in the following months.

Not long afterward, Logan appointed a team of attorneys for each of the defendants. Smothers was represented by public defender Guy Wilkerson and assistant public defender Billy Roe, both of Camden. Initially assigned to the public defender's office, Ramsey was slated to be defended by attorneys Dwayne D. (DD) Maddox, a well known and colorful West Tennessee defense attorney based in Huntingdon, and his son, Matthew Maddox. That change came after Roe reported to the court that there would be a conflict of interest in representing both Smothers and Ramsey—a clear indication that the defendants might be trying to implicate one another in some manner.

Logan appointed Steven West of McKenzie and Shipp Weems, a public defender from Dickson, to represent Harris. Weems contributed a lot of fireworks to the hearings in the months that followed. He was not as familiar with Circuit Judge Julian P. Guinn as the other lawyers were, as he practiced in a different judicial district, and thus was not quite as intimidated by the judge's reputation as some of the others might have been.

On several occasions, Weems pushed the judge's buttons almost to the breaking point—especially at a point where the attorney questioned the integrity of dying Tennessee Bureau of Investigation special agent, Alvin Daniels. Guinn more or less exploded after Weems moved that the judge recuse himself from hearing the case, stating that the judge's comments indicated a strong prejudice in Daniels' favor.

Indeed, an appeals court later took note of the comment

12

Weems protested. The court did not find the comment a reversible error, however, the justices indicated that they did not condone such statements made by a presiding judge.

The cold-blooded and grisly manner of young Brooks' murder generated a lot of anger throughout the entire county and beyond. Many people would have enjoyed seeing the trio dragged out of the jail and lynched, and street talk expressing such sentiments led Sheriff Brandon to worry that the three inmates in his charge might be in danger.

Further exacerbating the security problem were several phone calls from anonymous persons claiming that vigilantes just might remove the defendants from the jail. The sheriff was so worried, in fact, that, two days after their arraignments, he formally filed to have all three moved to the state penitentiary in Nashville for safekeeping.

At the outset of the formal hearing on the transfers, Brandon told the court that the threats had required him to pull patrolling road deputies in to provide additional security at the jail, a situation that could not continue indefinitely. Moreover, there were no funds in the budget for additional security beyond that. Brandon also worried about the safety of his personnel, should some violent attempt be made to remove the three.

Certainly, defense attorneys were not pleased with the idea of their clients being so distant from their office locations, as driving over two hundred miles round trip to meet with them would be a huge inconvenience. Both Roe and Matt Maddox argued that the transfers would hamper their ability to maintain sufficient contact with their clients. Maddox also noted that the state statute called for such suspects to be held in the nearest county jail facility and not the state prison.

Brandon said that the jail was overcrowded, which posed another problem. When Assistant DA Eleanor Cahill asked if there were concerns inmates might take some action against the suspects, the sheriff responded, "I'm not concerned about the prisoners doing anything. I'm concerned about the general public."

Under questioning by Harris' attorney, West, the sheriff acknowledged that the female section of the jail was not over-

13

populated, holding only three or four females at the time. There was also a single-person cell available in that section. Brandon said his main concern was that someone would overpower the jail staff and get their hands on the prisoners, reiterating again that his department had received threatening phone calls to that effect.

"Have there been any warrants issued for any persons threatening such action?" West asked. The sheriff said no warrants had been issued because he did not know the identity of those making the threats.

"Is it your testimony that widespread publicity has made the Carroll County jail insecure?" asked West.

"It's a good jail and we're proud of it," Brandon retorted.

The attorney then wondered if beefing up on the jail staff had made the facility as secure as it actually needed to be at all times. Brandon acknowledged that was true, but added, "We have to take the budget into consideration." The sheriff also admitted that he had not contacted other area county jails to see if he could locate one that was sufficiently secure, and willing, to hold the prisoners.

At the conclusion of the hearing, Judge Logan allowed the transfer of Smothers and Ramsey to the state pen and they were moved shortly thereafter. He denied the move for Harris, however.

"The problem here is, there's no overcrowding in the female section," Logan said, adding that Brandon could file for another hearing should some substantial threat to the woman's safety arise.

In the days following the hearing, the whole "vigilante" aspect of the security situation was shown to be something predicated on a "joke" by three lawmen. The three, two members of CCSO and one Huntingdon Police officer, admitted they had made the calls as a prank. All three received five-day suspensions without pay as punishment for their deeds.

The preliminary hearing for the trio took place on Monday August 23, before a packed house. Security was again tight as deputies used portable metal detectors on everyone entering the courtroom, and Judge Logan announced that those who left the

14

room during the proceedings were out permanently. Spectators carrying penknives or other sharp items were required to turn them over to the officers until the hearing concluded.

The number of young people in the audience was noticeably greater than the average trial. As it turned out, many of them were former schoolmates of the victim at South Carroll High School. Several of them openly dabbed at their eyes during the testimony as details of their friend's gruesome death emerged.

Assistant District Attorney Eleanor Cahill had handled the prior court actions in the case. Cahill was a tough prosecutor who could mix it up with any of the boys when the going got rough, as she had demonstrated many a time. However, with a case of this magnitude before the court, there was little doubt that the big gun himself, DA General Robert Gus Radford, would guide the prosecution with a personal hand. Thus, few were surprised to see General Radford seated on the state's side of the table behind a big pile of notes and files, flanked by Cahill and other staff.

"Gus," as he was known to all, was a formidable foe in any court. A rather large man with a disarming friendliness, he came across to witnesses as a man ready to understand anything. He had a slight stammer and perhaps he used it to advantage at times, giving the impression that maybe he was not keeping up with things well as he might have. But there was a steel-trap mind working all the time and, at the right moment, Gus would spring it and catch some witness under examination in a situation hard to explain. Moreover, he could come back with biting sarcasm when the opportunity arose.

Once, while questioning a woman whose husband, along with another man, was charged with robbing an elderly county resident, Radford inquired whether or not she had noticed anything strange when she arose the morning after the robbery. The woman said she had not really noticed anything unusual, although there *were* two sets of men's clothing in the living room floor that morning, which had not been there the night before. In addition, she noticed a sawed-off shotgun on top of the refrigerator. That gave Radford a perfect opening, as he turned toward the jury and smiled.

"Oh, I'm sure we all understand that," he said in all

15

earnestness. "We all get up and find strange clothing in the middle of our living room floor and sawed-off shotguns on top of our refrigerator." Several of the jurors unsuccessfully tried to suppress grins at that and at least one reporter struggled to keep from bursting out laughing. The witness could do nothing but sit there with a look of mortification on her face.

The purpose of a preliminary hearing is to ascertain if there is sufficient evidence of guilt to bind a defendant over to the grand jury and hold for trial. The state usually puts on just enough evidence to show cause to bind over and the defense rarely does more than cross-examine.

Radford's first witness was Carroll County Investigator Bunn, who was working the evening shift on July 30 and responded to the 1:31 a.m. call that came in from Keith Noles on Highway 114. The six-year CCSD veteran said he went to the scene and spoke with Noles and his wife, who reported hearing the altercation and gunshot. Noles thought he had heard two female voices, one of them cursing and demanding that someone lie down. Bunn checked the roadway and found spots of what appeared to be blood. Pieces of that asphalt were chipped up, bagged and sent to the TBI lab for analysis. There were blood drips down the road for about twenty feet, Bunn said.

Checking further around the scene, Bunn located a white pickup truck parked on the shoulder of the road about four-tenths of a mile away; he had passed the vehicle on his way to Noles' house initially. It was about 2:00 a.m. by the time he returned and the truck's engine was still warm. He estimated that it had been there an hour or so. A license tag was located inside the vehicle—which smelled of alcohol—and a record check indicated that the truck was registered to Ramsey. The investigator said that when Sheriff Brandon called him later that afternoon with the report of young Brooks being missing, he mentioned the broken pickup and added that things began to come together at that point.

The *real* break came with the discovery of Brooks' blue Ford pickup ablaze about a mile from Ramsey's house. Bunn detailed how he had been riding in the Henry County chopper searching along Highway 114 North and how he had spotted smoke rising from a field road around 4:30 that afternoon. A county fire unit was sent to the scene while the chopper landed at the county airport, where Bunn was picked up by Tennessee Highway Patrol Lieutenant Robert Earl Melton and transported to the fire scene. The investigator was informed that there was a body in the truck and observed it himself, immediately after which he phoned TBI Agent Daniels.

On the evening shortly following the grisly discovery, Agent Daniels and his crew set up at the county jail and began an active investigation. Daniels and two men from the state fire marshal's office gathered evidence from the burned truck, which had been moved to the jail impound area, while other agents went into the field to interview friends and acquaintances of the dead youth. Daniels said the truck's license plate had been found underneath the vehicle and a check of that and the VIN number indicated that young Brooks owned it. The remains inside were believed to be those of the missing man; that belief became reality once the body was transported to the state medical examiner's office in Memphis and dental records were compared.

The agent had come directly from his Camden home to Huntingdon when he received word of the discovery shortly after 7:00 p.m. With the leads pointing toward Ramsey, the 22-year-old was taken into custody at around one o'clock the following morning and transported to jail for questioning. He was too intoxicated for interrogation at that point, however. Daniels said that he and Special Agent Chris Carpenter did interview the man at 7:00 a.m. after he had sobered up sufficiently.

Ramsey acknowledged that he had been out with friends that night and that his truck engine had overheated and locked up. He said they had caught a ride home with a "black man in a black four-door car." He denied involvement in any crime, however.

Daniels, with twenty years of law enforcement experience under his belt, was well familiar with the ways and wiles of people who commit crimes. They cover up some things, but forget about others. Near the end of the interview, he asked to see Ramsey's shoes.

"Lots of times they'll change clothes, but they forget about

17

the shoes," he said.

Sure enough, there were red flecks that looked suspiciously like blood on the Nike sneakers Ramsey was wearing. That was easy to explain, the young man said—he had recently killed and dressed a deer. He gave officers permission to search his property and indeed a deer hide was located—one that was at least two weeks old, according to Daniels.

The shoes turned out to be a big factor in pointing the finger at the trio. Daniels said that during an earlier interview, Ramsey's sister claimed Deion Harris had given the shoes to Ramsey the previous day. Daniels knew somebody was lying at that point, but the matter was cleared up somewhat when Harris was questioned—she blurted out that the shoes were taken from the boy they had killed. Harris' off-the-cuff statement was made before she was issued a Miranda warning, however, and attorney West attempted to get it suppressed, a move that was overruled by Logan.

The shoes were identified by a member of the victim's family as having belonged to him, along with a number of other items taken from the home of Harris and Smothers. The recovered items were sent to the state crime lab for DNA and other testing, Daniels told the court.

A TBI agent and several deputies accompanied Ramsey to his residence for a search, while Sheriff Brandon and three agents went to the nearby house occupied by Harris and Smothers. Brandon said the woman was "very nervous, wringing her hands at the beginning," but that she calmed down somewhat finally.

Agent Daniels interviewed Harris on her front porch. She asked to move away from the doorway and further down the porch because she was afraid Smothers would hear her, the agent said. She also refused to sign a statement because "she was afraid Walter and them would see it."

The young blonde mother of two virtually sealed the trio's fate with the statement she made on the porch that hot July afternoon. She related how they had gone out in search of an ex-boyfriend who had been harassing her and how Ramsey's truck had broken down. She said Smothers had asked her to flag down a vehicle that was approaching and that Brooks had stopped. He was immediately covered by Smothers with the shotgun while Ramsey opened the pickup door and flung him down onto the roadway. Smothers then handed the gun to her to hold after he climbed into the truck bed, where he had forced Brooks, and she said that when she handed it back to him it went off, wounding the young man in the hip area. A little later, after they had driven away, she said Smothers shot the man in the head, killing him. She further related how the police had chased them in Hollow Rock and how they had eluded the officer. She had accompanied the two men when they took the truck and body to burn them.

All three were arrested on murder charges at that time and transported to jail. The following day, Sunday, August 1, Walter Smothers decided that he would make a statement. He told how the initial plan had been to bury the truck and body, but that a backhoe owned by Ramsey's family had a flat tire. He admitted they took some Mexican coins and a Sanyo radio from the victim and told officers where they could be found. Also found during the search were a bloody axe, shovel and two butcher knives, along with clothing Smothers and Harris were wearing the night of the murder.

Smothers admitted his prints were probably on the radio and commented, "I probably need an attorney."

"I said, 'Yes sir, you probably do,'" Daniels told the court.

The agent noted that Smothers' statement was much more detailed than that given by Harris. He claimed that the 20-gauge Stevens shotgun had gone off accidentally the first time after Harris handed it back to him and speculated that she must have cocked it; that type of external hammer, single-action shotgun will not fire unless the hammer is manually cocked. He did acknowledge firing the fatal shot under Brooks' chin as the pickup neared Hollow Rock, while the dying man pleaded for help.

According to testimony, Brooks' body was taken to another location for a planned burial before it was burned. The killer took officers to a spot on Parrish Road near Haunted Bridge.

Although it was generally known that the victim had been horribly mutilated, nothing of that nature was mentioned during the preliminary hearing. The nearest indication of the gruesome nature of the crime came when Daniels testified that Smothers had vomited while giving the "hideous" details of the crime and had done so again while at the Parrish Road location—which would later be revealed as the spot where the victim's body was hacked to pieces with an axe.

Public defender Billy Roe wondered if the agent had been concerned about Smothers' wellbeing because of the vomiting episodes. Daniels responded, "Counselor, if I was talking about what he was talking about . . . the man was telling me a very hideous thing and he got sick at his stomach."

The agent did acknowledge that Smothers had become visibly upset while giving his statement and that he "showed remorse" for what he had done. Daniels did not indicate how that remorse was expressed, however, and one might assume that Smothers was "upset" because he had been caught in a horrific murder that could lead him to the death chamber.

Indeed, at one point following his arrest, Smothers was transported to Methodist Hospital and given a shot for his "nerves." Roe later suggested that the situation might have been caused by Smothers' reaction to withdrawal from drugs and alcohol. All three had been heavily involved with drugs and alcohol on the evening of the killing and Smothers had acknowledged consuming Valium, tequila and beer.

During the lengthy hearing, defense attorneys made several attempts to have various statements suppressed, noting that some things had been said before Miranda admonitions were given. Matt Maddox questioned the validity of the search done on Ramsey's property, saying that the trailer searched belonged to the man's sister and that the defendant's mother had not given permission for a search of the barn. Maddox also told the court that a Paris, Tennessee, auto dealer had repossessed his client's pickup and that he intended to subpoena the company for access to the truck. Logan ruled that he would allow the vehicle to be held for up to forty-five days under such conditions.

The judge found cause to bind the defendants over, with a subsequent hearing scheduled for September 13, and he ordered they be held without bond. Neither of those rulings came as a great surprise.

And, again to no one's surprise, the grand jury indicted the three for a number of offenses, including felony murder. That became capital murder when DA Radford gave notice during the September 13 circuit arraignment that the state would seek the death penalty for all three.

Radford said the ultimate penalty for the trio would be sought by relying on three aggravating circumstances: that the murder was especially heinous, atrocious or cruel, in that it involved torture or serious physical abuse beyond that necessary to produce death; that the murder was committed for the purpose of avoiding arrest; and finally, that the murder was committed while the defendants were engaged in, or fleeing from, a robbery, theft or kidnapping.

Lawyers for all the defendants entered not guilty pleas as expected. Judge Guinn set October 13 as motions day, with September 23 the cutoff deadline for filing motions. He scheduled November 18 as appearance day.

Guinn said he intended to try to case sometime during the third week of January, pending any unforeseen delays. The judge's schedule was destined to go by the wayside, however, after Smothers made a deal with the state and trials for the other two were severed, with changes of venue allowed in each.

General Radford moved that the statements made by the three be removed from general sessions court and returned to the custody of the TBI. That came because Judge Logan had sealed the records at the conclusion of the August 23 preliminary hearing and *The Jackson Sun* newspaper had filed a suit in Carroll County Chancery Court against Circuit Clerk Paul Newmon in an attempt to gain access to the documents under provisions of the state's Open Records Act.

The *Sun* suit was heard Friday, September 3 by Chancellor Walton West, who indicated he would issue a ruling within fifteen days. *Jackson Sun* attorney Chuck Purcell told the court that the records on file with the clerk's office were subject to public disclosure and there was no reason to seal them. He noted that the decision to seal the records came after a side bar conference between Logan and Radford.

Attorney Robert Keeton, III, who represented Newmon, said the *Sun* had sued the wrong person, as Judge Logan—and not Newmon—had ordered the documents sealed.

"I don't think Your Honor has the power to place Mr. Newmon in contempt over a judge's orders," Keeton said.

The chancellor said that Keeton must show that Logan had the authority to seal the records and that if such happened, "I won't second guess (Logan)."

During the arraignment proceedings, Radford noted that general sessions is not a court of record and that the documents had therefore been entered in error. None of the defense attorneys had any objection to that motion.

"You draft an order that all statements be returned to the TBI," Guinn told Radford, in approving the motion.

That action would make the "Sunshine" lawsuit moot, as all TBI files concerning pending or open cases are excluded from public records. The judge's action merely delayed official acknowledgement of the sort of horrific injuries suffered by the victim, although media had learned of the mutilation via law enforcement sources and rumor that ran rampant within the community.

The reporter had been told by a law enforcement source, shortly after the body was discovered, many details of the gruesome mutilation; that information had come off-the-record with a promise not to reveal it. The obvious reason for the legal attempts to keep the horrible details of the crime under wraps was that they would further inflame feelings in the community and perhaps make jury selection far more difficult.

Along the same lines, Guinn granted a motion made by Maddox that 911 recordings in the possession of clerk Newmon be sealed. Guinn ordered that those recordings also be placed in the custody of the TBI, with defense attorneys to have access to the material upon providing reasonable notice.

The judge also appointed additional legal representation for the defendants. He said Dwayne (DD) Maddox would be appointed to assist his son, Matthew, in defense of Ramsey. He informed West that an assistant would be appointed for him in the near future. That turned out to be public defender Shipp Weems of Charlotte—a seemingly fearless attorney who became something of a thorn in Guinn's side as the case progressed.

Radford had some news for the court that did not greatly please Judge Guinn. The DA said DNA evidence being examined by the state lab would take 90-120 days and that autopsy toxicology tests would require an estimated four months. He said the TBI had made the case a top priority and was proceeding as quickly as they could.

"Set a fire under the state medical examiner!" the irate judge exclaimed. That schedule did not bode well for his previously stated intent to try the case in January.

Guinn then addressed the possibility of a change in venue, a situation made likely because of the nature of the case and the intense local media scrutiny. In one scenario proposed by the judge, the trial could be held in Carroll County, but a jury would be selected from another jurisdiction. Guinn said that possibility would raise an issue of where to conduct *voire dire* (questioning) of potential jurors. He asked defense lawyers to submit a brief memorandum with their recommendations.

The judge also noted that the state's intent to seek the death penalty in all three instances could lead to separate trials. He then posed the possibility of trying two of the defendants simultaneously, but with separate juries, each hearing only the evidence related to the defendant in that particular case. In another possible scenario, Guinn said that two simultaneous trials in different counties conducted by different judges might be possible, and that a third county might be necessary for the third trial.

"I would like the benefit of your thinking," Guinn told the defense attorneys, adding that he wanted only short memos and not lengthy briefs. Obviously, the logistics and costs were mounting up to a virtual nightmare, irrespective of what eventual path was taken.

Judge Guinn might have considered himself lucky when motions day rolled around on October 13 and he was tied up by another case. The other Twenty-Fourth Judicial District judge, C. Creed McGinley of Savannah, sat in for Guinn that day and faced, as McGinley put it, "a multitude of motions."

McGinley somewhat changed the scheduling order previously issued by Judge Guinn, allowing new motions to be submitted before a November 12 cut-off date. He set December 17 as a hearing date on those motions.

All together, defense attorneys for the three accused

submitted more than seventy motions, with West leading the pack with twenty-seven—one of those a big forty-pager in support of dismissing the charges against his client, Harris. Maddox filed twenty-five motions on Ramsey's behalf and public defender Wilkinson checked in with twenty-two, and a complaint that he had more to file but had not been given sufficient time.

Anyone doing a poll of unpopular people in society would soon find that lawyers are ranked right up there (or is it down there?) with aluminum siding peddlers and used car salesmen. They take a lot of heat because, in many cases, they are charged with the duty of defending the indefensible.

To the average layman, when a man admits that he placed a shotgun to a victim's head and shot him, there's nothing left to talk about. It is what it is—cold-blooded murder. First-degree homicide. Why go through months of effort, a forest of documents, hours of courtroom talk, thousands of dollars of expense? The man did it, so give him what he deserves.

But it doesn't work that way. As a nation of laws, and not of men, all those charged maintain the presumption of innocence until they have been convicted in court. A defense lawyer is obligated to give his client the best defense he can mount, short of suborning perjury or doing anything else illegal or unethical.

How does he do that? He looks for holes in the allegations, violations of his client's rights, laws that are possibly unconstitutional. He seeks to move the matter from places where it is well known to areas where possibly fewer people have heard about it and formed opinions. He tries to prove that statements were made under duress or some condition wherein his client did not understand his rights, if indeed they were even expressed to him. He requests bills of particular calling for state response in minute detail, motions in limine to prevent mention of past misdeeds. In short, he makes it as difficult as he can on the state while staying within his legal rights.

McGinley faced motions dealing with all those and many others that day, with many more to confront Judge Guinn down the road. Of those resolved during the hearing, many were conceded to by the state, such as all exculpatory evidence be provided to defense and statements of all witnesses be furnished—the kinds of responses actually required of the state in the first place.

As expected, the defendants asked for severance and separate trials for all, along with a change of venue outside of Carroll County. Also requested was that the state be prevented from any mention of prior convictions by any of the defendants; however, the defense would be allowed to introduce such evidence about the victim.

West filed a motion for compensation that would be reasonable in a capital murder case and for more travel expense; he requested travel money to attend the "1993 Death Penalty Litigation Seminar" scheduled at Nashville in late October. West also needed extra travel expense to visit co-counsel Weems' office in Charlotte, a two-hour drive.

One point of contention arose when Wilkinson said he felt discovery had not been forthcoming as well as it should have. Radford told the court that he would check and see what was outstanding, noting that he would provide all applicable discovery items directly to the defense attorneys when he received them, such as the lab and forensic reports.

"I strongly object," Weems interjected. "All that should be made a part of the record. The only way to properly review is if everything is filed in court."

That comment seemed to indicate that Weems was already thinking ahead to the appeals process, a point where the matter of official record is crucial for one attempting to ferret out errors and omissions.

McGinley said the state was under an order to file discovery directly to the defense attorneys and that it would then become part of the court record. However, he overruled the motion to have the material physically before the court prior to dissemination to the defense attorneys. In short, the court would not have to convene each time Radford received a new document pertinent to the case.

The judge established October 15 as the date for Radford to meet with and provide complete discovery to the Maddox team and to Wilkinson and Roe, and October 19 for a similar meeting with West and Weems. In a reverse discovery decision, he ruled that defense attorneys must also provide the state with any information regarding psychological or psychiatric examinations done on any of the defendants so the prosecution would have time to prepare proper responses.

Another motion from the West-Weems camp that seemed to indicate they were looking further down the legal landscape was one to require the state to respond to everything in written or narrative form. That would include all statements, whether in open court, chambers or electronically submitted, with all being preserved in a written transcript.

All the defense attorneys certainly realized going in that they had a long and difficult road ahead and, judging by what appeared to be the facts, one not likely to be successful when the case concluded. The more written record, the more chance of finding on appeal a vulnerability in what looked more and more like an airtight case.

General Radford took no position on many of the motions, as they were rote requests, but did take issue with several of the more pertinent ones. Foremost among those were motions to sever the cases—or have the defendants tried separately—and to change the venue of the trials. He told the court that nothing any of the defendants had said in their statements would incriminate their fellow defendants more than the fellow defendants' own statements; in short, that anything said about another had been substantiated by what the accused had said him or herself. As for defense claims that none of the statements should be admissible, the DA said the statements were taken in accordance with all laws and were admissible, and that all evidence taken, with or without warrants, was legally obtained.

As for a change of venue, the state's position was that no evidence had been submitted to warrant such a change. Radford noted that Carroll is a diverse county with a number of municipalities and that only once in the court's history had a change of venue been granted.

In what might seem amazing to the casual onlooker, one of the defense motions questioned the criteria for requesting the death penalty and asked for instances in which it had been requested during the previous ten years of the DA's tenure. Undoubtedly, anyone who believed in the death penalty at all would have had a difficult time finding a case in which the penalty would be more applicable, if the defendants were guilty.

Radford contended that the constitutionality of the death penalty was "firmly established in case law in this state" and cited three cases to support his position. He also cited three instances in which his office had sought the ultimate penalty since the most recent statute had come into play, including the aforementioned Housell case—which ultimately resulted in a second-degree murder conviction and a thirty-five year sentence.

The district attorney took greatest exception to the motion requiring everything to be filed in written form, stating that was not the general policy in that court.

"The state alleges the motion is made simply for the purpose of placing additional burdens upon the state and making the prosecution of the case more difficult," he contended.

Radford took no position on several items, leaving those to the sole discretion of the court. Among those were allowing defense attorneys additional time to file motions, and requests for reasonable compensation. He also conceded on a motion that would prohibit introduction of the defendants' past criminal records or evidence of prior misconduct. Such evidence would have no bearing on the charges at hand, but would surely prejudice jurors.

The DA opposed bond for Ramsey as requested by Maddox, noting the serious nature of the crime and the penalty sought. A brief hearing on that matter was conducted with TBI Special Agent Daniels as the lone witness. Daniels told about the bloodstained shoes recovered from Ramsey and said they had belonged to the victim. A 20-gauge shotgun believed to be the murder weapon was also recovered from Ramsey's property, he said. When Matt Maddox asked if Ramsey had admitted shooting Brooks, Daniels responded, "He did not." According to testimony during an earlier preliminary, Smothers had admitted being the actual triggerman.

In making his argument for bail, Maddox said the state had not proven the elements necessary to meet the criteria of capital murder in the case of his client, thus he should be eligible for bond. Judge McGinley disagreed.

"At this point of the case, I think the state has carried their burden," he said in denying the bond request.

Radford asked that the judge summarily overrule the motions for severance and a change of venue. His position was that, since none of the defendants' statements implicated the others more than their own statements, the trials could be conducted simultaneously. He said nothing had been shown to require a venue change.

McGinley opted not to overrule, but instead to allow attorneys an opportunity to file motions by the cutoff date stating specific reasons why the trials should be severed and the venue changed. Maddox saw a problem with putting in writing (and thus subject to public disclosure to the media) such reasons.

"There's been so much pre-trial publicity in this case that if I file in a written motion, I don't know what kind of affect it will have on my client." His complaint fell on deaf ears.

The judge also overruled defense motions challenging the constitutionality of the death penalty. He noted that higher courts had upheld the death penalty as constitutional under the current statute.

Weems came up with an unusual motion dealing with the possibility of a finding of guilt of his client, Harris. He said that if she were convicted, prior to the sentencing phase the jury should have to watch a video detailing the nature of death by electrocution. He contended that the statute called for "sufficient voltage," but claimed the State of Tennessee did not conform to that statute.

"It's capricious, cruel and unusual," said Weems of the state's manner of execution.

McGinley ordered Weems to submit a brief on the motion, since the matter referred to had not arisen under the new statute because no one had been executed in more than 30 years.

The next motions deadline arrived November 12 and saw defense attorneys file another gaggle of new motions, foremost among them thirty-three entered by Smothers' attorney, public defender Wilkinson. Weems filed only one—a request for expenses generated for travel, telephone and copying, which was summarily approved by Judge McGinley. Attorney Matt Maddox filed ten new motions, one of which sought to have his client

28

Ramsey joined to all motions filed by the other lawyers.

Murder trials in general create a lot of media coverage, and one so rare and gruesome in a rural area like Carroll County compounded that effect greatly. The defense seemed ready to go on the offensive against area media, as many of the motions considered in that proceeding had to do with attempts to gain access to reporters for a number of area papers and interview them, as well as to show cause for a change of venue.

Maddox and Wilkinson both filed numerous news articles from *The McKenzie Banner, Carroll News-Leader, The Jackson Sun, The Camden Chronicle, The Paris Post-Intelligencer* and *The Commercial Appeal.* Wilkinson sought to examine *Carroll News-Leader* reporter Karen Barker concerning her source for an article in which she wrote about a petition circulating in the community. Barker had it from a "reliable source" that the petition, which called for "justice to be served to the fullest extent", had been recalled so as not to complicate jury selection and a fair trial.

Another part of that motion, filed by both Wilkinson and Maddox, had an angle that seemed to indicate who they believed might have wanted the petition recalled. They moved to be allowed to examine General Radford about the matter, with Wilkinson citing an August 9 *Jackson Sun* story that alleged Radford had knowledge of the petition.

In his motion, Maddox said unfavorable articles about Ramsey were "circulated to incite the general public opinion against the defendant Ramsey and thereby deny the defendant a right to a fair and impartial trial by a jury of his peers."

The reporter was not mentioned by name during the proceedings, however, an article in the *Banner* written shortly before would prove to generate action by one of the defense attorneys not long afterward. That dealt with claims that Harris, incarcerated since July 31, was two months pregnant and had become so while in jail. There were allegations that sexual contact occurred among male and female inmates at the facility and that even some jail staff may have been involved. (In later years, both male and female jailers were convicted of participating in sexual acts with inmates and sentenced to jail time, although those cases had nothing to do with the Brooks murder case.)

The State of Tennessee has a "Free Flow of Information Act" or "Shield Law" which is designed to protect reporters from forcible disclosure of sources for information used in broadcast or written publication. This protection can be divested by a judge, but only if very exacting criteria have been met by those seeking to gain the information, via a three-prong test. They are: A) that there is probable cause to believe that the person from whom the information is being sought has info which is clearly relevant to a specific probable violation of the law; B) the person seeking the information has demonstrated that the information cannot be reasonably obtained by an alternative means; and C) that the person seeking the information had demonstrated a compelling and overriding interest of the people of the state in securing the information.

Only after a hearing in circuit court and a true finding of all three prongs can a reporter be compelled to reveal his or her sources—or face jail for contempt until they are ready to do so. Most reporters faced with that option usually take jail, because to reveal sources is tantamount to going out of the reporting business, especially for those who write news that sometimes depends upon anonymous sources, such as crime and government coverage. All such findings, however, are subject to the appellate court system and are automatically stayed pending appeal.

Most, if not all, reporters rely on anonymous sources at times. There are police officers and city employees and others who are willing to divulge good information a reporter would never obtain otherwise, but seldom are they willing to go on the record for obvious reasons. A good reporter will always try to find a second source or something to confirm such information before using it. And too, reporters must always be wary of people with self-serving motives or those with axes to grind in a personal fashion. It is a slippery slope and one trod with caution, the necessity for it aside at times.

People jailed on criminal charges very frequently discuss things with their cellmates, sometimes as braggadocio and sometimes out of guilt. Defense attorneys apparently believed

30

such had happened in the cases at hand, as motions were filed to exclude statements from Loretta Lynn Dudley, Jennifer Ann Williams and Pamela K. Baker, all cellmates of Harris. In the case of inmate Jeffrey W. Davidson, defense wanted to know of any threats or promises made to him in exchange for a statement he gave concerning an admission Smothers allegedly told him.

Motions for a change of venue were once again submitted, this time with a plethora of newspaper clippings and sworn affidavits from the defendants' families, contending that they had read and heard so much about the case that a fair trial locally was impossible.

Actually, merely having heard or read about a specific case does not automatically exclude one as a potential juror. The determination is whether one has made up his or her mind to guilt because of the publicity. In the cases at hand, it would seem likely that most people would form a presumption of guilt after having read that the defendants had given statements admitting their parts in the murder. Thus, it was not difficult to envision that a change of venue might be granted at some point before the trials began.

PD Wilkinson presented one motion that dealt with one of the law officers involved in the "vigilante hoax," Deputy Tommy Decanter. The public defender said Decanter had suggested to Smothers that he make a statement to Agent Daniels, and he wanted to know if there were any threats or undue influence used against his client. It became more of a concern, he said, since Decanter's actions had been instrumental in having Smothers moved from the jail to the state pen in Nashville.

Wilkinson also noted that Smothers had been under the influence of drugs and alcohol and on suicide watch when Decanter had initially approached him about giving a statement to the TBI. He suggested that the deputy used undue pressure to coerce a statement from the defendant.

Harris may have enjoyed a birthday party with all the trimmings "with the sheriff's blessing" while confined in the county jail, but Smothers was not getting the same kind of treatment, according to his attorney. Wilkinson filed a motion asking that the defendant be allowed a contact visit with members of his family, as he had seen his mother only once since his July 31 incarceration. The motion claimed that Smothers' three-year-old son had also become "visibly emotionally upset" in the absence of his father.

In addition, Smothers needed outdoor exercise for his health's sake, Wilkinson argued. Smothers had reportedly shown no indications of becoming violent since he was jailed, and in one instance even came to the aid of a jailer who was attacked by another scissors-wielding inmate, he said.

The motions were taken under advisement until they could be addressed by the judge. Judge Guinn's plan to try the case in January were by the wayside at that point. The only hearing before a February 16 statement suppression proceeding in Harris' case involved subpoenas issued to two reporters, including this writer.

There is one thing most news scribes dread worse than a terminal case of writer's block: a subpoena to appear in court and reveal the source of something stated in a news article. Faced with such a situation, and if compelled by the presiding judge to testify, a reporter has only two options: reveal the source(s) and forever blow his or her credibility, or refuse to testify and face contempt of court and jail until a change of mind occurs.

Reporters frequently opt for the second, because to reveal sources is tantamount to putting oneself out of the news business, let alone leaving one's integrity open to deep scrutiny. Therefore, when the reporter received his subpoena from CCSD Deputy Jimmy Simmons at the *Banner* office one morning, he knew in that instant that jail might definitely be in his future, depending entirely upon what transpired when the matter came to circuit court.

Steven West, the McKenzie attorney appointed by the court to represent defendant Harris, issued the subpoena. The document did not indicate what information West was seeking to obtain, but a phone call to the attorney quickly clarified that: he wanted to know the source of an allegation in a story concerning Harris, that she had gotten pregnant while held in the Carroll County Jail.

"Do you want to tell me who told you that and avoid the

32

court thing?" West asked.

"I can't do that," the reporter replied. "I gave my word. I can't break it."

"See you in court then," West replied, sounding as though he had a smile in his voice.

Truth was, the reporter felt somewhat *taken for a ride*. He had received that bit of information in an unsolicited phone call from someone he trusted—Dennis Brooks, the father of the victim. Brooks had told him that he got the information from a Tennessee Bureau of Investigation special agent; he did not say which agent, but the reporter believed that none of the agents would have told Brooks that were there not more than a grain of truth in it. It was, to use the old cliché, information he regarded as being "from the horse's mouth."

But, being good at what he did, he never liked to rely on one source without collaboration. Therefore, he put in a call to Douglas Brandon, High Sheriff of Carroll County and a man who had always been open and straightforward with him.

"Jim, I'm just afraid to say much about anything, with all this TBI involved," Brandon replied when asked about the pregnancy. "You know how it is with this sort of thing."

Indeed, the sheriff found himself in hot water several times during that period. At one point, he had allowed the family of Harris to hold a birthday party for her at the jail, complete with cake and balloons. The sheriff was soundly ostracized over the incident. There was a general feeling in the community that he was too easy on inmates in his jail to begin with and that "frosted the cake" for many. Truth was, Brandon was simply a nice guy who tried to accommodate people, sometimes to his detriment.

Brandon had never before hesitated to answer a question posed by the reporter if he knew the answer, although on some occasions he had requested that the information be withheld from print at that time. Therefore, his reluctance to address the matter added to the reporter's certainty that it must be true. It would not be a feather in his cap if some young woman became pregnant while in his jail, as it would substantiate the rumors of virtual sex orgies between inmates, and between inmates and staff that had flown for years. Indeed, one wag with insight into the jail operations had rumored about a sex orgy involving Harris and some trustees, wherein Harris allegedly "hung on the bars like a monkey" and had sex with someone outside the cell.

Of course, time proved that some of the rumors of that nature had no small degree of truth to them. A male jailer was later convicted of having sexual relations with a woman from McKenzie who was being held on drug charges. A female jailer was convicted of supplying marijuana and sex on a desktop to a young male inmate. Both were charged with official misconduct and perjury and served jail sentences, in adjacent counties, following guilty pleas on bargains worked out with the state.

After receiving the subpoena, the reporter went to his editor with the news. He was expecting to hear something to the effect that legal council would be obtained, but that was not forthcoming at that point. Therefore, the reporter decided he might as well attempt to draw up a response himself, and set about detailing a brief of his own explaining why his testimony should not be required.

It was obvious to even a legal novice that the allegations concerning Harris' pregnancy did not approach any of the three requirements to compel testimony, whether true or not. Yet, the reporter was not so sure Judge Julian Guinn would see it that way. Judge Guinn was a fair man, but he was rigid and unyielding—not to mention scary as hell when he went off on a lawyer, defendant or spectator, which he sometimes did.

The reporter had seen the judge call a witness to the front of the courtroom after a trial concluded and, in the presence of everyone in the room, tell the man what a liar and no-account he was. Another time in an assault case, Guinn told a sitting witness that he had never before seen such a pack of perjurers in all his career. Certainly one immune to defamation of character lawsuit can get away with such things, but such a display leaves an indelible impression on those witnessing it.

The rumor amounted to gossip in the larger picture and the reporter knew that. However, in the turmoil of the times and with the importance of the case, *everything* seemed to be fair game. After receiving the subpoena and pondering the possibility that he might wind up in jail if the judge ordered him to testify, the reporter questioned his use of the item and wondered if he had made a mistake.

Nonetheless, as he set about to write a brief addressing the subpoena, he pointed out that the effort to divest him of his journalistic protection did not meet either of the required prongs. He noted that he had at one time in the past had a verbal run-in with attorney West's wife at the police station over a police report concerning something that had happened at the lawyer's office, and that she had subsequently threatened him in front of witnesses at the *Banner* office.

Of course, he did not take those threats as anything but anger coming to the surface, but he felt the court might see some reason for West to have it in for him because of the incident. That did not seem likely, however, because Steven West had always been friendly enough, before and after the incident. But, at that point, the reporter was looking for anything to hang his hat on in the legal sense and the verbal altercation might help his case.

The following Wednesday, he ran his homemade response past Judge Logan for an opinion. Logan said it "wasn't bad," but pointed out a problem area.

"You need to take all this personal stuff out," he said, referring to references of past problems with the attorney's wife. "That has nothing to do with the case and the judge probably won't look upon it kindly."

Having no desire to test the mettle of Judge Guinn, he began to revise the document. Thankfully, that proved unnecessary, as Editor Joel Washburn advised him that a well-known First Amendment lawyer from East Tennessee, Richard Hollow, had been hired to represent the paper during the upcoming hearing. Hollow was scheduled to fly in to the Carroll County airport in his private plane on the morning of the proceedings.

That most dreaded of mornings came and the reporter was filled with trepidation, uncertain as to whether or not he would be a free man later in the day. Hollow arrived as expected and came to the courthouse with Washburn. There, he told the reporter that he did not think the judge would rule that he had to testify, but that if he did the reporter would be facing a difficult decision. "He can put you in jail until you decide to talk," he said. The reporter replied that he was willing to go to jail if it came down that way, because he was not going to reveal a source.

The lawyers did what lawyers do, a lot of talking. West claimed that the information was critical to the defense and put his client in a bad public light with untrue publicity. Hollow said the report did not meet any of the requirements necessary to compel a journalist to divulge sources. Even District Attorney General Robert Gus Radford took a stand that the information being sought by West had nothing to do with the pending case against Harris.

"It wouldn't matter if Chandler said she had buck teeth," Radford told the court. "It has nothing to do with these murder charges. Now, if she wants to pursue something in civil court, that's a different matter."

That latter comment caused the reporter a bit of consternation, as being sued for libel was second place on the lists of things reporters do not wish to experience. He was wishing Gus had not given them any ideas, although he realized that a libel suit against him would likely prove fruitless.

Teresa Harris had become a public figure when she was arrested for murder, thus merely making a misstatement about her would not constitute libel. It would have to be made with malice or reckless abandon for the truth. The reporter was certain that he could provide a multitude of witnesses—including most of the court officers and attorneys—who could testify that he paid great attention to getting things right, more so than any other reporter who had ever covered proceedings in that courtroom. Still, the expense and time required by such lawsuits were unpleasant to ponder.

A scribe for the Huntingdon-based *Carroll News-Leader* was also in the courtroom under subpoena. She was not represented by legal counsel, but as it turned out she was able to ride the coattails of the firm that *had* hired legal representation.

Judge Guinn took the matter under advisement for a brief time and then came back into the courtroom. He ruled that the information being sought did not show cause to breach the state's Shield Law and thus the reporters would not be compelled to testify.

There was certainly an audible sigh of relief at that point, emanating from a very nervous reporter sitting near the front of the courtroom.

The year 1993 ended and '94 rolled around. It became obvious that the initial timetable set by Judge Guinn would not be met. Defense attorneys had the unenviable task of defending clients who were "sure as sin" guilty and so employed every tactic known to the criminal justice system in an effort to give their clients the best defense possible. They are required by law to do so, even if those clients have damned themselves with statements made to authorities.

Judge Guinn granted severance of the cases and set trial for defendant Harris during a Monday, February 14 hearing. He said the woman's trial would begin March 23, with those of Smothers and Ramsey to follow in that order. A change of venue had been granted at a January 28 hearing and, as of that time, all the trials were expected to be held in neighboring Henry County. Defense attorneys expressed some doubt about using Henry County because of its proximity to Carroll and because of publicity in the Paris paper and area TV news broadcasts covering the situation.

During the February 14 hearing, motions by defense to suppress statements went by the wayside in two of the cases. Judge Guinn ruled that the statements taken from Smothers and Ramsey would be admissible, however, he deferred judgment on Harris' motion until Wednesday. She was ordered to be transported back to Western State Mental Health Facility directly from the court. The defendant wept and trembled uncontrollably while in the courtroom and was unable to walk at times without the assistance of a female deputy. A doctor summoned from Bolivar by defense attorneys Weems and West arrived Monday afternoon and examined Harris.

"I believe she is in a state of disassociation at this time, disengaged from reality," Dr. Phillip Morson told the court. The doctor told Radford that he believed the woman should be hospitalized and that she was not competent to testify.

The move from the courtroom back to Bolivar was Harris' third trip to the mental facility. She was first sent January 15 after an attempt to hang herself in her jail cell. Harris spent seventeen days in the hospital that time, but was later transported back to the hospital after concerns arose that she might again attempt suicide.

Judge Guinn ordered the transfer back to the hospital until a February 16 hearing, two days hence, on Harris' statement suppression. He said it might become necessary to move her to the women's prison hospital in Nashville if more treatment was required.

The problem with Agent Daniel's health, and the possibility that he might die or become totally disabled before the trial began, generated another dispute during that court session. The agent's health was severely in decline by that point as he underwent chemotherapy for cancer. Attorney General Radford said he wished to have the agent make a statement that day for the purpose of preserving his testimony, as he might not be able to further appear in court. Radford furnished a doctor's statement to support that possibility.

Harris' attorney, Weems, immediately objected to preserving the agent's testimony on constitutional grounds, stating that his client was not present to cross-examine. Radford countered that Weems had been advised prior to allowing his client to return to the hospital that Daniels would be called for the purpose of preserving his testimony for the record. If Weems believed he was going to get some slack because his client was not there to face her accuser, he was sadly mistaken.

"Go on and make your record," Guinn told the district attorney, overruling Weems' objection.

Attorneys for the other two defendants then made similar objections to allowing Daniels to testify. Guinn quickly overruled those objections without any discussion.

DD Maddox arose and informed the judge that Ramsey' defense would refuse to participate in questioning Daniels because they were waiting for psychological test results that would have an impact on their line of questioning. Wilkinson and Roe indicated they likewise would refuse to cross-examine the dying agent. Guinn said he would consider motions March should the results of psychological tests have some bearing on the testimony given by the agent, but he did not stop Daniel from testifying for the record.

The agent, appearing ashen and almost bald from the chemotherapy, detailed how Harris had "blurted out" a comment concerning where Ramsey had gotten the bloodstained sneakers while being questioned at her home. She was given her Miranda warning at that point and then she gave officers permission to search the residence, which turned up a number of items connected to the crime.

As for a comment Daniels made to Harris on her porch that if she was "going to talk now is the time," the agent told West that it was simply an investigative technique designed to obtain information. He acknowledged that might lead the woman to believe he could be of some assistance to her.

Indeed, the authorities are within legal bounds to lie to persons being interrogated for the most part, so long as they do not wander into pure old coercion. They are not allowed to extract a confession by threatening to kill a loved one if one does not confess to a crime, but they can claim they will provide assistance that they cannot provide, or claim there are witnesses who do not exist. Such subterfuge plays a large part in gaining confessions in many cases.

Attorney West wondered if Harris was being detained prior to her arrest. "If she came out with a bag and said, 'I'm going to Mexico' would you have stopped her?" he asked.

"No, I had no reason to at that point," Daniels replied.

Sheriff Brandon, who accompanied agents to Harris' home, saw things a bit differently. When West put the question about letting her go to Mexico to him, the sheriff replied, "No, I don't think so."

Deputy Decanter, whom Wilkinson had earlier believed had some part in coercing Smothers into making a statement to Daniels, was also called to the stand. Decanter had known Smothers as an acquaintance since junior high school and was on duty when he was brought in following his arrest. He said he checked all three defendants on a 20-minute basis, as they were under close watch as possible suicide candidates.

To Wilkinson, he denied he had told Smothers he was "into it this time" and needed to talk to Daniels. "I did not tell him to give a statement," said the deputy, who had served a five-day unpaid suspension for being one of the prank callers.

There had been rumors circulating for some time about a possible "deal" forthcoming for one of the defendants. A comment made by DD Maddox seemed to indicate that something might be in the air—but apparently not for his client. He said Ramsey was slated to stand trial last, but that might change if the other two defendants were not tried for whatever reason.

On February 16, 1994, two days following the hearing in which Guinn ruled that statements given by Smothers and Ramsey would stand, a hearing was conducted in circuit court to address a motion by Weems to suppress Harris' statement. That initial statement given by Harris had set the ball rolling on the arrests of all the participants.

There was always a bit of extra excitement in the courtroom when Shipp Weems appeared before Judge Guinn. The judge was a former naval officer and maintained that disciplined bearing. Always well dressed and sporting a neatly trimmed full black beard, though somewhat short in stature he nonetheless cut an imposing figure.

The reporter's first real contact with Judge Guinn had come during the Housell murder case in 1986. He had stopped the judge in the hallway and questioned him about some of the judge's instructions given to potential jurors in that case, comments like "nobody purports news articles to be true" and that some things were just "made up."

The reporter had no knowledge of the judge and his stern reputation and was not afraid to address him, though he did so with respect. He told the judge that he did not make things up; had he wished to do that, he would not spend a day sitting on the hard bench in a courtroom. Guinn was cordial enough, replying that some reporters did have "axes to grind," and that the real evidence in a trial was presented from the witness stand, and not a newspaper. There was no arguing with that contention, certainly.

Weems was something of a character himself. With his grey hair and tweed jackets, he looked like a man who would be quite at home as a university professor. Weems came from a long line of achievers in Tennessee and was related to former Governor

Frank Clement. His great-grandmother, Agnes Work Shipp, was the first woman elected to public office in Tennessee, that being superintendent of schools of Dickson County in 1895. She thereafter became librarian for the State of Tennessee.

His grandmother, Dockie Ann Shipp, was something of a genius and was licensed to teach in any school in Tennessee at the age of 14, after obtaining degrees at Dickson Normal College and Vanderbilt. Besides becoming an educator, she went on to become well known as a public speaker and established her own school to teach the art.

The centerpiece of Weems' motion to suppress the statement Harris had given to Daniels in July was the defendant herself. Harris was transported back to Huntingdon that morning from Western State Mental Health Center in Bolivar, her third trip there in recent days. She was taken directly from the courtroom on Monday, two days before, appearing to be on the verge of hysteria.

The petite blonde, still appearing as nervous and near out of control as she had throughout the entire process, acknowledged that she was on medication, but said that it did not affect her judgment or hamper her recall of the day she gave the statement. She said the appearance of so many armed men at her home, and the separation from Smothers that day, had frightened her into making the statement.

Weems was leading the witness so overtly during these comments, drawing them painfully out of her one at a time, that DA Radford finally objected. He was sustained by Judge Guinn.

One of Harris' main contentions was that Daniels had threatened her. "He (Daniels) told me I'd better tell the truth or I'd fry in the electric chair," the distraught witness told Weems. Daniels had not admitting making such a comment during the Monday hearing, but had said he told her she needed to tell the truth, which was simply an investigative technique. Weems had another name for it.

"They are implied threats. I submit they amount to coercion," he said.

Weems also noted that while the TBI agent had claimed his client was not officially detained, the sheriff had seen things in a different light, contradicting the testimony of two agents.

"I recall," said Judge Guinn, dourly. "You put the line in his (Brandon's) mouth and he bit."

Guinn's comment appeared to indicate that Weems had somehow tricked Brandon into disputing the testimony of the agents. And yet, most observers might have found it highly unlikely that the officers at the scene would have merely stepped aside had Harris packed her bag and announced a sudden trip to Mexico, or anywhere else.

Weems asked Harris if the officers had promised her anything in return for making a statement.

"I don't think so, they just told me to tell the truth and they would help me any way they could," she replied in a trembling voice.

DA Radford pointed to armed bailiff Wayne Kirk and asked if he made Harris nervous, as she claimed the officers' guns had the day of her initial interview.

"Yes, I stay nervous," she replied.

The witness admitted to the DA that when officers first spoke to her, she knew that Ramsey's truck had been found and she knew that Ramsey had told the authorities that Smothers was with him the evening it broke down. She also acknowledged that she had signed a permission to search form and had told officers about certain items in the residence.

Weems argued that since his client had been detained and not Mirandized before making the initial statement, the statement she made after being read her rights was illegal and should not be admissible, nor should anything derived from it—what's known as "fruit of the poisoned tree" in legal circles. Radford countered that officers could detain a person for a reasonable amount of time while investigating a crime and that her statement was freely and voluntarily given.

Not surprisingly, Judge Guinn agreed with Radford. Moreover, as for any problem with the veracity of Agent Daniels, well, Guinn was not going to hear it. The judge said he had known the dying agent for a number of years and had seen him testify on many occasions, and had found the man's integrity beyond question.

"Particular care was given to protect this woman's rights by Agent Daniels," Guinn said emphatically. "You couldn't beat a lie out of him!" He then overruled Weems' motion to suppress the woman's statement.

The defense attorney was on his feet immediately following that ruling.

"I would ask that Your Honor recuse himself, based upon Your Honor's statement about Mr. Daniels," said Weems.

Guinn wasted no time denying that request. He informed Weems that he could make that motion in writing if he wished, but indicated that he would also overrule such a written motion.

Attorney Weems was not deterred by Guinn's expressed position on refusing to disallow Harris' statement and the physical evidence in her case. When the next hearing rolled around March 8, he was back at it again with yet another motion to suppress both the statement and the evidence collected after she spoke with authorities on her Dillahunty Road porch that Saturday in July.

Addressing the motion required another appearance of Agent Daniels. The agent appeared far more ill than he had during the previous month's hearing when his testimony was taken to preserve the record; it seemed doubtful that Daniels would survive long enough to see an end to the trials.

On the stand once again, the agent admitted that Teresa Harris had been upset, crying and trembling, when she was questioned and made her statement.

"Did that bother you in any way?" Weems inquired of the woman's emotional state.

"No, most of the people we deal with get nervous and upset," Daniels replied. He said Harris' "conscience could have been bothering her" to explain the state of her mind at that point.

"There was something wrong with her for whatever the reason?"

"Yes," Daniels replied.

Daniels testified that Harris had signed a search waiver authorizing him and Agent Chris Carpenter to search the house, a 1983 Thunderbird, and all other outbuildings on the property. The purpose of the search was to gather items she had already told officers existed in those locations. She was given her Miranda rights before she signed the waiver, he noted.

43

Had she refused to sign the permission, the agent said he would have gone to a judge and gotten a warrant. He would have instructed the other officers to stay on the location until the warrant was in hand.

Another new motion brought by Weems and West, and the Maddoxes for Ramsey, addressed what the state would be allowed to say about possible mutilation of the victim's body during the upcoming trials. All the attorneys contended that any mutilation done to the victim *after* his death was not relevant to the charges pending against their clients and should not be used as an aggravating factor.

The idea of suppressing those gruesome facts did not sit well with DA Radford. He said proof would show that young Brooks was dead when the desecration happened, but contended that the mutilation was a continuing phase of the murder and as such was relevant.

"If you limit the state's case to the murder itself, it's going to take away eighty percent of our case," Radford told Guinn. "Otherwise, they just held somebody up and shot him."

"I think the jury is entitled to have the complete facts," Guinn said in overruling the motion to suppress mention of the mutilation.

At one point in the hearing, DD Maddox quoted from a bill of particulars several distinct examples of physical desecration done to the victim's body. Radford immediately objected to the disclosure, saying that he was under the impression the information was not to be placed into the record or made public at that time. The judge agreed.

Weems then gave the court notice that he intended to construct an insanity plea for defendant Harris. The lawyer said he did not think he could prepare his case by the established trial date of March 28, because he was going to seek further psychological evaluation and expected different results from those gathered by the latest tests.

Radford opposed any change in the schedule. He said that nothing in the current mental evaluations indicated the woman met criteria required to raise an insanity defense.

"A person in her spot would normally be depressed and maybe have suicidal thoughts," said Radford. "If given enough

44

time to go to enough psychiatrists, one will say what (Weems) wants to hear."

"I've got a feeling the general is going to be talking out of the other side of his mouth when the reports come in," Weems retorted. "I don't think he wants to go to a capital murder trial with a local psychiatrist as his only witness."

Judge Guinn agreed with the district attorney. "In all candor, Mr. Weems, I don't see any reason I can't go to trial March 28," the judge said in overruling Weems. Undeterred, the defense attorney immediately again requested a continuance and was again told by Guinn that the case would go to trial March 28 as previously stated.

The Maddox team representing Ramsey made another attempt to suppress his statement by calling a Nashville psychologist, Pamela Auble. The woman testified that she had examined Ramsey and found him to be "not a very intelligent individual." She based her findings on a battery of tests administered February 11.

According to Auble, Ramsey's IQ was 81, or at the bottom of the low average area. His reading skills tested at the fourth grade level and his vocabulary was "very poor," she said. She described the man as a "dependent individual who is kind of immature" and said he was the kind of person who could be influenced easily by others—a "people-pleaser kind of person who just wanted to be successful and be liked."

"I think I have that," quipped Radford with a grin. "I like to please people, be successful and be liked, too." Judging by the expression on Auble's face, that last one probably was not happening.

Auble acknowledged to the DA that reading ability was not directly linked to intelligence, however, she said it was an indicator and correlated with it. She could not speculate about which words in the Miranda warning Ramsey might, or might not, have been able to comprehend.

Ramsey took the witness stand and admitted that he had understood the Miranda admonition and what his rights were. It was uncertain whether that ready admission was a backlash to Auble's low opinion of his intelligence, or proof of it. He said that he had graduated from Huntingdon High School in 1990 with average grades. He had believed it was in his best interest to speak with the TBI agent before talking to an attorney.

"I wanted to tell him (Daniels) what happened, because I had not killed anybody," the lanky young man told Radford.

Radford acknowledged that the evidence would show Ramsey was not the triggerman who fired the shotgun. That fact would have no bearing on the charges, however, since all participants in a crime of that nature are equally responsible irrespective of who does what.

Oddly enough, public defenders representing the man who *did* fire the fatal shot, Smothers, did not present any motions that day. The reason would soon become apparent—Smothers had cut a deal with the state to testify against his cohorts in exchange for a life without parole sentence. That turn of events infuriated many in the community and had some people questioning what "justice" was.

Conversely, there were those who believed that life behind bars without the possibility of parole was far more punishment that a few years on Death Row and then a quick ride in "Old Sparky," the state's electric chair—which had not been used in more than thirty years anyway. Moreover, the deal gave the state about an airtight a case as any district attorney has ever taken before a jury.

The long-awaited first trial in the Dennis Brooks Jr. murder kicked off Monday, March 28, some eight months after the killing. Teresa Deion Harris was set to go before a jury of her peers at the Henry County courthouse on the square in Paris. By the nature of the case, and with a possible death sentence in the offing, selection of those peers could prove to be a lengthy and involved process.

As usual in all parts of the proceedings up to that point, security was very tight. Sheriff Douglas Brandon and a cadre of his deputies were on duty at the courthouse in the adjacent county and a number of personnel from the Henry County Sheriff's Department assisted them. Feelings in the community still ran high and it was obvious that the officers were not going to allow anything to jeopardize the safety of the defendants before justice was legally delivered in a court of law.

Dressed in a blue floral frock, the defendant appeared very nervous as she sat at the table beside attorney Steven West. She did appear to calm down somewhat as the day progressed, however.

All during the proceedings, past and future, it was not unusual to see either West or co-counsel Weems pat the young lady's shoulder or make other attempts to comfort her during the very stressful moments. It was obvious to any observer that the lawyers were sincerely concerned for Harris' fragile emotional state.

Indeed, just looking at the young woman one would never imagine she could be involved in something so heinous. She was petite, blonde and shapely; pretty in a girl-next-door way. It was said that she came from a good family of decent people, but it was also known that she had lived a troubled life in many ways.

There was alleged sexual abuse when she was younger, marriage and babies too soon, mistreatment by a number of men she had known, a descent into drugs and alcohol. Like so many, she had fallen through the cracks and become a victim of sorts herself, destined never to know much real success in life even with the criminal charges aside. Hers was a story played out repeatedly in places large and small, a story destined to end badly simply because of bad luck, misfortune, and a host of poor decisions.

None of that, of course, justified in any way what happened to the 19-year-old man on a lonely and dark stretch of Highway 114, a man whose decency had allowed him to fall for a ruse that claimed his life. One could only think that, pretty exterior aside, Deion Harris had to be an ugly monster on the inside.

Anticipating difficulties in seating twelve jurors and two alternates, Judge Guinn had an additional third panel of prospective jurors summoned. That would provide a larger than normal pool of 155 from which a valid jury might be drawn. The additional bodies filled the small courtroom, already at capacity, well beyond that. There was a front row bench assigned to the media, however, thus a number of news people in attendance would have access to everything that happened.

What the court wanted to do was find forty qualified jurors from the pool. That would allow for twenty-three preemptive challenges by both defense and state and still leave enough to seat a jury and alternates. Once selected, the jury was to be sequestered, reportedly at the Best Western motel. Some wondered if locking the jury up over Easter holiday might not cause problems; Judge Guinn indicated that testimony in the trial would continue into Saturday if necessary, in an effort to avert that if possible.

Early in the Monday morning selection process, Judge Guinn gave prospective jurors something of a history lesson. He traced the jury system back to the time of the Magna Carta in the year 1215, when King John had assured everyone the right to a trial by jury. Guinn called jury service "one of the greatest experiences of citizenship."

Obviously, there were quite a few who would disagree with that assessment, people who had other things more important to do. More than a dozen offered reasons why they could not participate, but only a handful bearing proper medical documentation were excused. The judge said work-related considerations and old age were not justifiable reasons for exclusion according to the rigid state law under which he had to operate.

The initial examination of potential jurors Monday morning was limited to two areas: the amount of pre-trial publicity to which jurors had been exposed, and their feelings on the application of the death penalty. Called into the jury box in groups of six, they faced intense questioning by DA Radford and defense attorney Weems. All seemed to have heard something about the case, however slight, and none voiced opposition to the ultimate penalty. Of the first three groups of six questioned, fourteen persons were found suitable for the jury pool.

One man, an employee at the Bruceton rail yard, said he had formed an opinion of the case and would not be able to set it aside no matter what the evidence was. He was dismissed, as was another man who had similar misgivings. Another young lady, one who had initially been found acceptable, was dismissed after she told the judge that she had a planned singing engagement the following day.

The judge stressed to the prospective jurors that everything they had read or heard via the mass media was "hearsay" and not based on facts.

"Newspapers are in the business of selling newspapers," he said. "No one purports it to be facts," adding the same was true of television and radio. His comments were reminiscent of the Housell case and the discussion the reporter first had with Judge Guinn.

If the judge had little use for the media, it was possible that he had even less for Mr. Weems, chastising the man on several occasions for his manner of questioning. He ordered Weems to "move on" and at one point said the defense attorney was "beating the subject to death" in an attempt to instruct the citizens about the law.

"Mr. Weems, quit instructing them in the law. *I'll* instruct them in the law," Guinn said in no uncertain terms. A short time later the judge declared, "You're trying to put words into that lady's mouth!"

Weems, who had wanted to read a list of possible mitigating factors to jurors but had been prevented from doing so by Guinn, retorted, "I disagree with the judge."

"I've ruled upon that issue," said Guinn, in a way that suggested it might be wise to move on and stop disagreeing with him.

At another point a short time later, Weems said he and the judge had a disagreement over the word "fact," after the judge had stopped the attorney from using that word in reference to media accounts. The judge had already stated how he felt about news accounts and he quickly informed Weems that, "there will be no disagreement."

Weems and West had entered another motion over the preceding weekend again asking for a continuance, although Guinn had ruled at the last hearing that the case would proceed as scheduled. Guinn summarily overruled Weems' latest motion just as he had a number of other motions on the same subject.

Judge Guinn did permit Weems to give a brief explanation of mitigating factors, after one juror said he could not assess what effects such factors could have if he did not know what they were. Mitigating factors were anything that might tend to lessen the severity of punishment should Harris be found guilty, such as her young age, lack of criminal record and a diminished capacity to appreciate the severity of her crime because of mental disease or intoxication. Weems stressed that jurors might hear certain facts during testimony that would prove to be mitigating factors.

It took several days to seat a jury composed of six men and six women, and testimony began for real on Monday, April 4. One of the early surprises came when DA Radford announced that a plea bargain had been reached with defendant Smothers and he would be testifying for the state against his former lover.

In announcing the deal, Radford said the Brooks family had been consulted and were in agreement with the arrangement. Indeed, Dennis Brooks later said that the family had agreed because the triggerman's testimony was somewhat crucial in proving the case. It was never addressed as to why, with so much condemning evidence, including the statements of all the defendants, it was necessary to make such a deal with the man who actually killed the victim. It obviously made the cases against both Harris and Ramsey ironclad, however.

Even more surprising was the fact that during Harris' sentencing hearing, the father of the victim mounted the witness stand on behalf of the convicted killer of his son. In that instance Brooks said the family had determined that, "We don't want the Harris family to have to suffer the agony we've suffered," thus their motives appeared purely altruistic.

In his opening statement, DA Radford laid out what the evidence would show during the coming trial. He detailed the dates, the scene and what the state would prove occurred during the time in question. Evidence would show that the trio stopped Brooks, who was "house-sitting" his grandfather's home at the time, after their truck broke down. They would take him brutally from his truck and place him in its bed, after which he was shot the first time.

"The proof will show that she still had the gun when he was initially shot in the side, hip and leg," said the DA. The Brooks family was weeping quietly by that point in the statement.

Radford went on to detail all the other actions of the trio as previously mentioned. He said the woman's statement to authorities was not altogether true, as she had tried to shift blame to others.

"At the conclusion, we will have proved to you that Teresa Deion Harris is guilty of first-degree murder of Dennis Brooks, Jr.," Radford concluded.

In his opening statement, defense attorney Weems called the upcoming testimony "a journey in search of the truth" and said the jurors would be "confronted with many horrors." Weems stipulated to the fact that Dennis Brooks, Jr. was dead and said, "We will relive the last hours of his life on earth."

Weems said the state's eyewitness would be the man who shot Brooks in the hip and then, as he begged for help, "his face was blown off by another shotgun blast." Weems said the man who had done that had his life spared because he was testifying against his client. Radford objected and was sustained by Guinn.

"Walter Smothers, to what crime does Walter Smothers answer?" asked Weems. "As I stand before you today, I do not know."

Weems told the jury that the evidence would show that his client was "at the wrong place at the wrong time with the wrong people." He said she had no intent to commit a crime and had no knowledge that Smothers intended to take anyone's life, or commit any of the other crimes involved.

Radford opened his case with the testimony of the dying TBI agent, Daniels. He related how he had entered the case and what he had found upon reaching the site where the body and truck were found. He said that because of the fire and mutilation done to the victim, it was not initially evident that it was a human body. The burned truck was placed on a car-hauler and transported to the jail impound area with the body still inside to help preserve the evidence, he said.

Daniels testified that he requested the help of other TBI agents and it was after daylight before processing of the truck was finished. The body parts were removed and fragments collected and sent to Memphis for autopsy. While it was not officially known then that the body was that of Brooks, the TBI was acting on that assumption and began to interview friends and family of the missing man, he said.

Daniels detailed how he and Agent Chris Carpenter had interviewed Ramsey, and told of the bloodstains visible on his black and white high-top Nike sneakers. The agent said he talked to Harris on the porch of her home about the shoes.

"She said they were the boy's shoes, and they killed the boy," he told Radford. Daniels said Harris was given her Miranda rights at that point.

The agent then detailed the entire scenario as acknowledged from the statements of the defendant, from the stop to the shooting, chase through Hollow Rock, and the later disposal of the body and truck. At one point reading from the statement, Daniels related that Harris had said, "All I could hear was the axe chopping." Shortly afterward, Smothers said, "Let me show you how to do this," and stabbed the body. "I stabbed him once in the stomach," Harris said in the statement. She told how Smothers had amputated the victim's penis and placed it back into his underwear because, "He might need it someday."

Daniels said Brooks had been robbed of $13 and some "old Mexican coins" according to the statement. "Ramsey took the shoes off the boy's feet," Harris told him.

Forty-three items were introduced into evidence during Daniels' testimony. A Sanyo AM-FM cassette radio, stolen from Brooks' truck, along with two Mexican coins and a Grover Cleveland coin, were entered. There were pictures of some items entered and Daniels said the axe "with blood all over it" that Sheriff Brandon had found in the well shed was still at the state lab.

The 20-gauge Stevens shotgun recovered from Ramsey's trailer was also introduced. Daniels, also a certified firearms instructor, noted that the single-barrel weapon had to be manually cocked before firing—indeed, indicating that no one could be accidentally shot with the weapon unless it was put into a dangerous Condition 0 configuration, which is loaded with a round in the chamber and cocked. That type of single-action firearm has no additional safety.

DA Radford questioned Daniels for about two and a quarter hours. After lunch, West got the opportunity to cross-examine the witness. He asked Daniels to turn to the last page of the statement and tell what Harris had said to Brooks after the gun had fired the first time. The agent replied that she said she told the man to be quiet and maybe he would not get hurt any further. As for the gun, Daniels acknowledged that it would have to be breeched open and reloaded before it could be fired again.

Daniels detailed again how Ramsey had been too intoxicated to interview when first picked up. He was a suspect at that time because of the location where his truck was found, and witnesses in Yuma had also placed the trio in the truck that night, he said. In addition, there was Noles' report of the disturbance near his home and the bloodstains on the highway not far from Ramsey's disabled truck. Ramsey implicated Smothers in the crime during his initial interview when he had sobered up sufficiently that morning, the agent said.

When asked about the shoes Ramsey was wearing, Daniels responded,"I thought they belonged to Ramsey." He said Ramsey's sister had said Harris had given her brother "her boyfriend's shoes"—it was not clear if that was supposed to be a reference to Smothers, or her earlier boyfriend, Hampton.

Several agents were already at Harris' house the day he and Sheriff Brandon arrived, Daniels said. One of them told him there was something wrong and he suspected Harris was the "weak link" in the situation. He acknowledged that he told Harris "now was the time to talk" before she made her admissions. She was not given a Miranda warning until after she had made the statements about the shoes and said, "They shot the boy." She was very nervous, trembling and upset at the time. Daniels denied that he said he would try to do what he could for her.

The agent also denied that he used any extreme threats to the woman and said he used the same tone of voice in which he was testifying that day. It was Harris' idea to move down the porch where Smothers could not hear her conversation. She asked at some point if she was going to go to jail.

"I told her yes, she probably would," said Daniels. He said Harris refused to sign a written statement because she was afraid Smothers or Ramsey would see it.

"Did her statement assist you in arresting the other two?" asked West.

"Yes, sir," said Daniels.

Radford objected at that point and Judge Guinn called a side bar conference with the attorneys. A short time later, another side bar was called after Radford objected when West questioned whether Daniels had spoken with Harris' mother and sister at the jail following her arrest. Daniels said that he had spoken with Harris' relatives, but had not told them she would receive help because of her cooperation.

"I said I wouldn't resist a bond if one was set," said Daniels. The ill agent admitted that he had been up all night, for more than thirty-six hours in fact, when he spoke with Harris' family at the jail.

DA Radford's next witness was the victim's father, 48-year-old Dennis Brooks, Sr. A tall, large man with coal black hair, the anguish was evident upon his face as he took the stand and began to tell of his family in response to Radford's question. For some reason, the defense objected but was overruled by Judge Guinn.

Brooks, who operated a landscape service, said he had lived in Huntingdon for nine years after moving from Memphis; at some point, he said he left Memphis because of the crime there. He lived with his wife and 17-year-old son Jeremy, while daughter Sheila lived in Memphis and another daughter, Stacy, lived in Little Rock. Dennis Jr. was living at his grandparents', Charles and Mary Brooks', vacation home near Hollow Rock just to keep it occupied and to keep an eye on the place. Brooks explained that his parents only occasionally stayed at the house; on holidays and sometimes over weekends.

The witness said his son was a student at Jackson State Community College and had planned to transfer to Memphis State. Weems objected on the grounds that Brooks' testimony was not relevant, but was overruled. Brooks said he had last seen his son when the family all went to Memphis for a funeral. "We found him a little truck," the man said emotionally, almost breaking down. He said the application for a loan was approved with the credit union and his son was supposed to buy the truck on Friday.

At that point, the witness was openly weeping. Shortly, he regained control of his emotions enough to continue. He said his son had supper with his grandmother, Mary Ann Parkinson, that Thursday evening. He was supposed to come by the elder Brooks' house the following Friday morning to see about getting the truck. In fact, Dennis Jr. had called around 10:00 p.m. Thursday evening to say that he would meet up with his dad the following morning to finalize the deal.

"Did he show up?" asked Radford.

"No sir, he did not," the witness replied, his eyes wet with tears.

Brooks said that when his son did not arrive as planned he began to look for him. He drove out to the farm and found no signs that the boy had even been there the previous evening. At that point, he returned home and called the sheriff, who launched the search. He said because of the winding road, he had been fearful that his son might have struck a deer and had an accident.

Radford asked how Brooks had learned his son had been killed.

"Three young friends of his came to my front door at 12:30 Saturday morning and told me they had heard it on a police scanner," he sobbed in reply. By that point, several jurors were having difficulty controlling their emotions, as were a number of people in the audience.

Brooks had been shown a number of items removed from Harris' house during the search. He said his wife's father gave the Grover Cleveland coin to his son, but he didn't recognize the two Mexican coins. He identified the Nike Air Jordan shoes taken from Ramsey's feet as his son's and said there was a sales slip from the Old Hickory Mall where they had been bought on April 9. Weems again objected, but was overruled. He identified a tool pouch with several tools and the radio; he had installed the radio in his son's truck and the box it came in was in his basement.

"Have you stayed in close contact with the district attorney and law enforcement?" Weems inquired under cross-examination.

"Yes sir, I talk to them," Brooks replied. He said he knew when charges were filed, but that no one had confessed in his presence.

"Have you been advised they have (confessed)?" inquired Weems. DA Radford objected at that point and requested permission to approach the bench. After both attorneys held a side bar with Judge Guinn, Weems indicated that he had no further questions for the witness.

Huntingdon Subway manager Mary Dill testified briefly. She told the court that young Brooks had worked there five or six weeks. She said she spoke to him at 12:30 a.m. on that fateful morning—about an hour or so before he was killed. He had called because he was worried that the money was not checking up right. He was closing and preparing to leave at that time. To West, she acknowledged that she had no idea what had happened after Brooks left the sandwich shop.

Next on the stand was David Hampton, the man who might have been the victim had things gone differently that night. Hampton, who did not know Brooks, told Radford that he had dated Harris for about a year and a half and had broken up with her in July, around the time she began seeing Smothers.

Hampton said he had called and spoken with her that day about the coat. He had offered her $50 for the coat. He also spoke to Smothers and things were friendly enough. However when he changed his mind about paying the $50 and called back things went a bit sour.

"Me and Walter had some words," said Hampton, adding that the argument only involved threats of fighting, and not killing. He said he was not aware that anyone was planning to come to his house. In fact, the trio was about a quarter mile from his house when they abducted Brooks, but Hampton did not hear the initial gunshot.

The witness said he saw all three defendants on Highway 114 the next day. They had the hood up on a white pickup and the men were looking at the engine. He noticed Harris' Thunderbird parked alongside the road and she was sitting in the

56

driver's seat, he said. That was around noon. He was going to the store for smokes and did not stop or speak to them—probably a wise decision, considering what had happened earlier that day. The white pickup was gone about four hours later when he passed the location on his way home.

Hampton told Weems that he had met Harris through her ex-husband, Jim Harris. He said they had lived together for about a year before the July breakup. When asked if Harris knew how to get to his parents' home where he was staying, Hampton said Harris knew where they lived. "She went to my parents' house millions of times."

Hampton again related how he had called back that second time around 9:00 p.m. to tell Harris he had decided not to give her the $50 for the coat.

"What kind of reception did you get from Walter?" asked Weems.

"He told me he was going to kick my ass," Hampton answered. He said Smothers had wanted to meet him on the coming Monday—Smothers had previously made the comment about Monday being a full moon, which he apparently thought was a good time to fight or kill. "I guess to duke it out," said Hampton concerning a Monday meeting.

The man said he really did not know Smothers, other than having met him a couple of times at parties. He also did not know Ramsey, although he had seen him while living with Harris.

Weems inquired if Harris had ever attacked him in any way.

"Several times," said Hampton.

"Didn't she have to go to the hospital two times?" asked Weems. Hampton said he could only recall once, that for a sprained ankle and a knot on her head. It was not made clear if Hampton was responsible for the injuries, although that seemed to be the implication.

Under re-direct by Radford, Hampton said there might be no reason to fight but he and Smothers had agreed to anyway. Moreover, it could be said to be over Harris, in a way. Radford asked about the fights he and Harris had engaged in when they lived together. Hampton said Harris had once come home drunk from the Fish Fry (an annual spring festival) and had fallen off the porch. She was throwing things around in the house and calling him all sorts of names. Another time, she threw all his clothes in the yard and then stomped all over them.

"Why did you stay with her?" asked the DA.

"I have no idea," Hampton replied, shaking his head.

Weems had a couple more questions for the witness. He asked if Hampton had ever struck anyone besides Harris. He said he had not. Hampton acknowledge that he had used the same foul language as Harris had, but said he did not commonly use such words and did so only when angry.

Keith Noles, the man whose early morning phone call to the sheriff's department about the late night disturbance on the highway near his home got the ball rolling, was next to testify. A rural mail carrier, Noles had lived at the house on Highway 114 between Buena Vista and Westport since 1983. He said Hampton lived about a mile from him, which was somewhat different from what Hampton had earlier testified.

Noles' house sits about seventy feet from the road and there are bushes in front. He said there were no lights on at the house the night of the incident. He and his wife were sleeping on the enclosed porch because of the heat and he woke up thinking he had heard voices. He said he looked out the window and could see the taillights of a vehicle shining through the foliage. He lay back down, but could hear voices.

"I heard a male voice say something about ten dollars," Noles told Radford. "Let me have ten dollars, let me borrow ten dollars, something like that." Then, he heard a male voice say, "I've got it covered, I've got it covered," and the engine of the vehicle revved up. Someone then yelled, "If you move the truck, I'll blow your goddamn head off! Do you hear me?" A few moments later, Noles heard a gunshot and what he thought was a woman screaming.

"I could hear a woman's voice yelling, 'Lay down motherfucker!' as the truck took off," Noles said.

He got out of bed and dressed, then walked down to the road where the vehicle had been parked. He spotted what looked like blood on the blacktop.

"I don't believe they (deputies) believed me," said Noles, adding that the first officer there thought the fluid looked like "transmission fluid." When Investigator Bunn showed up, he agreed that the substance was blood, however, Noles added.

Noles said he had seen two men and a woman by a broken down white truck later that day. The woman was grinning and had her hands on one of the men's waists, he said.

Noles told defense attorney Weems that the male voice speaking of the ten dollars had not sounded aggressive. He said even the "I've got it covered" did not sound aggressive, nor did the "I'll blow your head off." He acknowledged that would be an aggressive thing to say to anyone, but said it did not sound that way.

"I didn't take it serious," said Noles.

The "do you hear me?" an instant later was a different matter. That was said in a very loud and aggressive voice, and was immediately followed by the gunshot and screams. Noles said at the time he did not believe the "female" voice making the scream was the same voice he had heard talking.

"I thought it was a bunch of drunks that had stopped to use the bathroom," said Noles.

Radford came back and asked Noles if the person doing the screaming could have been a 19-year-old shot in the side with a shotgun. He gave as an example someone like singer Wayne Newton, who had at one time had a very high-pitched voice for a male.

Noles shook his head. "I've thought of it several times and I'm sure it was a female voice," Noles answered.

Noles' wife, Jonnie, related essentially the same story. She said her husband had woken her and said, "I think somebody is fixing to get shot." She then heard the shot and the yelling and then a lot of mumbling or talk that could not be understood. She did think that the voice demanding someone lie down sounded "very hateful." She said she still heard that voice at night.

"Stuff like that just don't happen," said the woman, shaking her head.

Hollow Rock Police Chief Tommy Bridges took the stand shortly before four o'clock that afternoon to tell of his brief part in the tragic scenario. Bridges said he was patrolling on Highway 70 at about 1:30 on the morning of July 30 when he crossed the junction at Highway 114. He spotted a vehicle traveling at a high rate of speed and turned around and gave pursuit. The pickup truck turned north and he lost it, he said.

Bridges told Radford the incident was not logged at headquarters because, "We don't log it when we lose them." He said he had heard about the report Noles had made to the sheriff's department.

The chief told West that the time was approximately 1:30 or 1:40 a.m. and he had heard about the call Noles made over the police radio.

Stephen Gooch of Yuma and a friend had been parked in front of the old post office in that community on the night of the murder when they had an encounter with the trio. Gooch said a white pickup with two men and a woman in the middle pulled up.

"The truck was knocking pretty bad," Gooch told Radford. "They had wanted a quart of oil but we didn't have any."

Gooch said the truck came from the direction of Westport and left out the same way. He saw the same truck alongside Highway 114 a couple of miles from Westport the next day. He did not recognize the people in the truck that night in Westport.

CCSO Investigator David Bunn became involved in the case immediately upon Noles' early morning call to the sheriff's office. He was on duty in his office at the time and was notified of the call by the dispatcher. He, along with deputies Cary and Smothers (also named Walter Smothers, but no relation to the defendant) headed to Noles' home.

Bunn said that while en route, he saw a white pickup parked alongside the road and stopped to check it out. The hood of the vehicle was still warm, indicating that it had not been there for very long. A check of the license plate and VIN number indicated that the truck was registered to Stacy Ramsey.

Once at Noles' place, he spoke with the man about what had precipitated the call and was shown the substance on the roadway. Deputies chipped up and bagged samples of the bloody tarmac for examination by the state crime lab.

Bunn said that later that day, around two-thirty to three o'clock that afternoon, Sheriff Brandon informed him of the missing man. Helicopters were requested at that time and Bunn said foul play was suspected in the disappearance. He was aboard one of the choppers and spotted smoke arising from a field, and called in the fire crew. Bunn estimated the distance from the spot near Noles' home where blood was found to the site of the burning truck at about nine miles. The burned truck was a little more than one mile from Harris' house.

"It looked like it was a corpse in the truck, but we couldn't tell for sure at the time," said Bunn. "I knew it was some kind of animal."

At that point, the investigator called in Special Agent Daniels. The scene was sealed and secured and the truck was removed to the jail impound so the body could be removed there.

Bunn told Radford that he was at Harris' house later when the search was conducted. He said he and TBI Agent McLean chipped up concrete there containing spots of something resembling blood.

Defense attorney West inquired as to what time Daniels had been called into the investigation. Bunn said that happened around 6:00 p.m., shortly after the truck and body were discovered. He said he told Daniels about Noles reporting what he believed to be a female voice screaming during the incident near his home. Harris was questioned about ten on the morning of July 31 and he did not know at that point that she and Smothers had been at the scene near Noles' home.

Officers had been to Ramsey's home about three hours prior to questioning Harris, however. That was because of the connection with his pickup found near the scene of the incident reported by Noles. Bunn had not been aware initially that Harris and Smothers had been with Ramsey.

Ramsey was arrested shortly after Harris was interviewed. Bunn said he assumed at the time that was because Harris had confessed—which he later learned was the case. Bunn told West that he had been present during the interview with Smothers when the man admitted shooting Brooks in the head.

West immediately objected to the admissibility of Smothers' statement admitting the shooting. After some discussion, Judge Guinn ruled that he would not allow the statement entered "at this time."

TBI Special Agent Steve Champine then testified briefly about his part in the investigation. Champine, who normally worked Obion and Weakley counties, said he went to Ramsey's trailer around noon on the 31st and participated in the search. He found the 20-gauge shotgun propped in a corner behind a TV. He was present during Harris' questioning later and opined that she was "coherent."

Champine told West that when he initially went to Ramsey's, he had no information that the other two had been in Ramsey's truck the previous evening. It was suspected that Ramsey might be involved with the burned truck and body, however. Since Noles had heard multiple voices, it was safe to assume that more than one person was involved.

Champine said that after speaking with Harris, he believed she was hiding something and he relayed that suspicion to Daniels.

"I thought she was being deceptive," he said, adding the she appeared at the time to be the weakest of the three.

"Did you hear anyone else say they shot Mr. Brooks?" West asked. Radford immediately objected and was sustained—Guinn had already ruled that Smothers' statement was not admissible at that point. West, obviously trying to get into the minds of jurors as early as possible that Smothers had admitted the actual killing, tried to reword the question, but was again shot down by another sustained objection. Judge Guinn was simply not going to allow the confession to be entered at that point, but it was soon to come. The next morning, in fact.

The state led off Tuesday morning with its star witness, Walter Steve Smothers. During his stint of more than two and a half hours on the witness stand, Smothers coolly related the details of the kidnap and bloody slaughter of the young victim.

At times, the witness looked toward members of his family sitting in the courtroom and smiled. He acknowledged, upon questioning by the DA, that he had agreed to accept life in prison without possibility of parole in exchange for his testimony—a fact that would seem to indicate he had little to smile about.

According to Smothers, he had known Teresa Deion Harris since he was 10 or 12 years old and they had begun dating in June 1993. They had met at bars and parties around that time and "sort of wound up together." He moved in with her at her Dillahunty Road home about a week before the murder.

The witness said that Ramsey lived in a mobile home directly across the road from Harris. He did not know the man until the day of the murder, but met him after Harris sent her son over to ask Ramsey to "come smoke a joint" with them. Later, the trio ventured off to Paris, where they purchased a fifth of tequila and a 12-pack of Budweiser beer. Returning home, they drank the whole fifth in about half an hour and consumed beers and several Valiums.

The problem started that evening when David Hampton, one of Harris' former boyfriends, called. There was an argument about the coat. During a couple of calls Hampton made about the coat that evening, he got Smothers the last time and an argument ensued. Hampton had agreed to give Harris $50 for the coat, and then changed his mind.

Smothers told the court that Hampton wanted to fight him and he was supposed to meet the man; he was not certain if the meeting was supposed to be that evening or another time, however. The witness said he would have preferred to wait until Monday to fight "when the moon was full," since it was not yet full that Friday.

"We decided to go that night," said Smothers of his showdown with Hampton. He did not like the fact that the man had beaten Harris and put her in the hospital once, or so Smothers contended.

The three loaded up in Ramsey's pickup—after first getting his 20-gauge Stevens shotgun—and set out to find Hampton's home in the rural Yuma area. Harris was the only one who knew the directions, as she had lived with the man and had been there many times. The woman dropped off her son and daughter at her former mother-in-law's home on Northwood Drive in Huntingdon. The trio then purchased gasoline at a convenience store on East Main before heading out.

Once out in the countryside in the south county area around Yuma, things began to go south on several levels. Not only could Harris not find the correct road leading to Hampton's place, but the truck began acting up, running rough and knocking. Harris later claimed that she knew the road but had kept it to herself for fear Hampton would be killed.

The truck was running so poorly that they attempted to buy crankcase oil from two boys they spotted parked near Yuma, but were unsuccessful. They finally decided to give up the search for Hampton's house and head home while the truck was still running, however, the engine locked up on Highway 114 several miles outside Hollow Rock.

Stranded there along the dark road, the trio drank what beer they had left and discussed their situation, according to Smothers. They decided they would take the next vehicle that came along.

"What were you going to do with the driver?" asked Radford.

"We'd probably have to kill whoever it was," Smothers replied. "I don't know. We were all messed up."

They knew that it might be difficult to get someone to stop along the isolated road after midnight, so it was decided that Harris would be good bait because she was "young and pretty." Smothers said he and Ramsey hid behind the disabled truck while Harris stayed in view to flag down whoever happened along. She fully knew what the plan was, the witness said.

Like most decent young men who spot a damsel in distress, young Brooks did not hesitate to stop when he saw Harris motioning at him along the darkened road. One can only imagine the terror he surely felt moments later, as Smothers and Ramsey ran around the pickup armed with the shotgun, screaming at him. Smothers had the shotgun and he ordered the man out of the truck. Ramsey grabbed Brooks by the arm and flung him down onto the road, where Harris struck him several times.

"She said, 'Lay down, motherfucker, lay down!'" Smothers told the jury.

Brooks was ordered into the truck bed and told to lie down. During the process, Smothers said he handed the gun to Harris, who covered the young man with it through the sliding rear window. Smothers then took the gun back and it fired.

"I reached to get the gun, when Stacy speeded up suddenly. I latched onto the gun and the gun just went off."

The load of number four shot struck the victim in the area above his hip, creating a horrendous wound. Later medical testimony would indicate that the shots pierced the liver, intestine and bottom lobe of the lung, also severing several major arteries. It would have eventually proven to be fatal, as the young victim was bleeding to death internally.

"He started screaming, real high-pitched, like a woman or a bobcat," said the killer. The Brooks family was understandably in such an emotional state by this point in the testimony that the bailiff had to take a box of tissues to them.

As the truck sped on toward Hollow Rock, the injured man continued to cry and plead for his life. At one point Smothers told Brooks that they were taking him to the hospital, a complete lie. As they approached town, the streetlights became evident. Brooks obviously noticed that and began to scream with renewed vigor, perhaps hoping someone would hear him in the more populated area. At that point, Smothers cast his last shred of humanity to the winds.

"Somebody said shoot him or something, or I heard it inside my head," he said.

"Did you shoot him?" asked the DA.

"Yeah, I shot him. I stuck the gun up to him and shot him, under the chin."

Dennis Brooks, Jr. made no more sounds after the shotgun boomed across the sleeping landscape for the second time that morning. About 120 miles to the southwest, in Memphis, his grandfather Charles bolted upright in bed. It was 1:30 a.m., he noticed, and something had jarred him from his sleep, leaving him with a foreboding feeling.

"I don't know if he was trying to tell me something or what," the elderly man later told the reporter, before his emotions got the best of him. "He was my hunting buddy. He was a good boy."

Once in Hollow Rock, the murderous trio ran into a bit of a problem. Smothers explained how the police car had spotted their speeding truck and how they had managed to evade a stop. The three drove back to Harris' house and parked around back. They talked about how they were going to get rid of the carnage in the truck bed. They came up with a plan to use a backhoe on Ramsey's property to bury everything—truck, body and all. A flat tire on the implement shot that brilliant plan down, however.

They decided to just bury the body and Ramsey got an axe and a shovel from the well house, Smothers said. He got a screwdriver to remove the radio from the truck, while Harris fetched a butcher knife from the kitchen. When shown one of the two butcher knives previously introduced as possibly used in the mutilation, Smothers said, "I thought it was bigger."

He proved to be correct, as Harris later testified that neither of the knives displayed in court were used to stab and mutilate the body; however, a larger one not taken by law enforcement had been. Smothers had washed the knife at the kitchen sink following the brutal act and placed it back with the other cutlery.

With all the tools necessary to dispose of the body at hand, they once again left Harris' residence. Ramsey and Smothers were in Brooks' red Ford Ranger and Harris followed in her 1983 Thunderbird. She would provide a ride home, because they intended to leave the pickup. They came finally to a spot on Parrish Road, a gravel road of about two and a half miles in length that begins at Thompson School Road and ends at the Browning Highway. A bridge along the short route is called "Haunted Bridge" and is a location where youths congregate at times to hang out, drink beer and smoke dope.

Weems entered an objection when Smothers' testimony came to what happened to the body at Haunted Bridge. Judge Guinn sent the jury out of the room and allowed both sides to make an argument. Weems said that any testimony about the disposal of the body was not relevant to the crime and that entering it could prejudice the jury so substantially that they could not fail to bring back a first-degree murder conviction. He said that Smothers should not be allowed to testify that Harris participated in the disposal of the body.

Radford countered that prosecutors had always been allowed to show culpability of a defendant. He said it was relevant as to her state of mind to commit a crime and her participation in the act.

Weems told Guinn that was true in some cases, but said there was no evidence Harris participated in the disposal of the body.

"Chances are, he (Radford) wants to poison the mind of the jury with horrible facts," said Weems. "She can't get a fair trial."

Guinn sided with the district attorney, stating that Harris' involvement was obvious because she was present when both shots were fired. "I'm going to let the testimony in," he said, ordering that the jury be returned to the courtroom.

Once at the bridge, there under a moon turning full, the trio fell under the spell of complete blood lust. With the single-bit axe in hand, Smothers began to chop at the victim.

"I cut off one of his legs, Stacy cut off the other," he said casually. He said that he then cut off one of Brooks' arms; a medical witness later testified that the bones had been "broken" by the dull axe and not cleanly cut.

Harris was having her part of the bloody ritual as well, according to Smothers. He said she stabbed the body a number of times with the butcher knife. Smothers could not recall whose idea that had been, but they all took turns stabbing the body with the big butcher knife.

Harris claimed that she stabbed the body only once and then because Smothers had told her to do it. Forensic experts testified that the body had been stabbed at least six times in the upper torso area, which could be determined by cut marks on the rib bones. There could have been more wounds not striking bone; however, the burned condition of the remains made it impossible to say.

One might wonder how such a horrid scene could get worse, but it was about to. The victim's penis was cut off and his heart was removed.

"Deion said she wanted his heart," said Smothers.

"Did you get her the heart?" asked Radford.

"Yeah, I cut his chest open and got his heart," said Smothers. "She stuck it up to her mouth. I'll never forget the look in her eyes when she asked for it." Smothers' last statement about the look in her eyes caused the only hitch in his voice during his entire testimony, as though the look had made some everlasting impression upon him in a way all the other carnage had not.

Moreover, it would later come to light that the heart had been passed around and kissed by all three of the killers, and not just Harris. It was one of the several indications that "devil worship" had played some part in the ritual aspect of the killing.

With time slipping away from them and morning light soon coming, they decided to abandon the burial plan and simply burn the truck and body. They returned to Harris' house in the T-bird and obtained a five-gallon can of gas and some oil. They then drove the death truck to an area off Langford Store Road and down a field road a short distance. Harris waited in the car while Smothers and Ramsey piled the victim's remains into the cab, soaked everything with fuel and then set it ablaze. From her waiting spot on the road, Harris could see the flames lighting up the dark morning sky.

Back at the house, all three took showers to wash away the blood and gore. Harris washed the clothing they were wearing. The woman would later tell a jail inmate that no matter how many showers she took, she could never wash away the haunting smell of that brutal evening. Perhaps, as a psychologist would later relate about the recurring nightmares and posttraumatic stress syndrome suffered by Harris, the smell would become nemesis locked forever in her mind, a harbinger of her own form of living death behind walls and fences, a place she would leave only after her eyes closed for the last time.

Smothers and Ramsey woke up in Harris' car the next morning—why they were in the car, he was not sure. They drove out to where the broken pickup sat on Highway 114 and discovered that it had suffered a blown head gasket. Using one of his father's vehicles, Ramsey towed the broken truck home.

Smothers could not remember every detail of that day because they had continued to drink and take Valium. At some

68

point in the afternoon, around three o'clock he guessed, they did return to where they had left Brooks' truck and found that it had not burned to their satisfaction. It was set ablaze again and not too long afterward was spotted by Bunn in the helicopter. Ironically, the trio might have remained free somewhat longer had they not made it so easy to locate the missing vehicle.

Smothers and his ladylove did go to Casey's tavern in Huntingdon that evening. She was sporting a blue and white Memphis State ball cap—a cap that had last been owned by a young man now in pieces and recently found smoldering off a field road. According to the tavern owner, she appeared to be in a chipper mood, singing along to the jukebox and "bopping around" more than usual. High on alcohol and drugs, the long, slow descent into hell had not yet begun.

Later that night, the trio made up their alibi story, most of which was concocted by Smothers. The truck had broken and they had caught a ride home with a black man driving a black car.

It was a tale that might have fooled a slow six-year-old, and they tried it when the men in suits and ties showed up at the house the following day. It did not hold up long.


After the man laid out his testimony for the state, it was time for defense attorneys to have a go at him in an effort to punch some holes in his story. McKenzie attorney Steven West, a redhead with a sort of tenacious bearing himself (the same fellow who had caused the reporter grief with his subpoena) saw some flaws in what Smothers now claimed in comparison to his original statement.

For one thing, Smothers had originally said that Harris had handed the shotgun back to him before it went off. Now, he was saying that it was still in her grasp when he reached for it and it went off.

"It's not the same statement if that's what you're asking," Smothers told the attorney, explaining that after thinking about things for some time, some of it had become more clear in his memory.

West also pointed out that there was no mention in the original statement about a discussion among the three concerning taking a vehicle or harming the occupant.

"You remembered that after the plea bargain, isn't that true?" asked West. "Was that because of Deion's original statement at the house that got you arrested? Didn't you say at the jail, 'If I'm going down, I'm taking everybody with me'?"

"I'm not positive I said that. I remember parts of it real well."

"And that's the parts that tend to lay blame on others, isn't it?" the lawyer countered.

When asked if he had already pleaded guilty, Smothers replied in the negative. West then inquired when he would enter such a plea.

"I guess at the first opportunity," the witness replied.

"The plea is conditioned on you testifying here today?"

"That's my understanding," said Smothers.

The defense lawyer then asked Smothers if he had not said that night, "Don't worry about it, it's not the first one I killed."

"I *know* I didn't say that," Smothers replied emphatically. Smothers claimed that he did not intend to shoot Brooks when the man was stopped and that he said, "We *might* have to kill somebody," not that they definitely would.

Harris would later testify that Smothers seemed so well versed in the killing that she believed he had committed murder before. She also alleged that the man had told them they would have to kill again in two days—apparently because the moon would be full at that time.

Smothers told West that he had begun drinking late in the afternoon on the day of the killing, around four to five o'clock. He was drinking beer but could not remember exactly how many. He took two or three Valiums and smoked some marijuana, then drank tequila after they went to Paris and purchased the fifth. He was not sure if he took more Valium, but probably did. When asked where all this took place, the man answered, "The place I was staying. I would call it *home*."

West inquired again about how many beers Smothers drank during this time.

"I don't keep count of 'em, when I empty one I get another," Smothers cracked wise.

The defense attorney wondered why Smothers' recollections from the stand seemed to be more complete than the information he gave to Daniels in the initial statement and another made February 24 following the plea bargain. Smothers answered that as time had passed, he had dwelled on what happened and gained more insight into it.

"Did that have anything to do with whether you would go to the electric chair?" asked West.

"It's not the same statement if that's what you're asking," Smothers retorted.

West then had the defendant read from parts of his statements and questioned some of the things omitted from the earliest one. The attorney said there was no mention in the initial statement about any plot to take a vehicle or harm the occupant and suggested Smothers had "remembered" that after being offered a plea bargain.

According to Smothers, he had not been particularly upset with what Harris had told Daniels on the front porch, even though her revelations had ended with his arrest.

"I wasn't overwhelmed or nothin', it's a part of life," he stated philosophically, no doubt beginning to realize that his fate was sealed and that, essentially, his life was over.

The state called on a number of other witnesses in an effort to build an airtight case against the defendant. Among them was O.C. Smith, an associate professor of pathology at the University of Tennessee Medical School and the state medical examiner from Memphis who did the autopsy on the victim.

Smith, who cut something of an odd appearance with his closely cropped hair, dark suit and tie and black high top lineman boots, would have his own future legal problems several years hence. He was charged by federal authorities with staging his own abduction, wrapping himself with wire and planting a bomb on himself. A federal trial on those charges resulted in a hung jury and the man eventually returned to work as a state pathologist.

The pathologist detailed for the DA the injuries inflicted upon the body that he had received on the morning of July 31. He said both shotgun wounds were "severe" in nature, but said there was no way to determine which had occurred first. He said the head wound would have "immediately rendered a person immovable and unconscious," however. He noted the amputated limbs and stab wounds in the torso of the burned corpse, and said that all had taken place post mortem, or after death occurred.

Tests conducted on the body revealed no drugs or alcohol present in the system. Identification of the body was made by dental record comparison. He could not ascertain height and weight because of the damage done to the victim. Blood and tissue samples, along with the shotgun wadding removed from the body, had been submitted to the TBI for further testing, he said.

Under cross-examination, Weems questioned whether or not "torture wounds" were present upon the body. Smith replied that any sort of wound could be a torture wound, depending upon the circumstances under which it was afflicted. He added that three stab wounds to the liver showed some evidence of bleeding, but the bleeding could have resulted after death. He was certain the larger trauma—the hacking and burning—had been committed post mortem.

Radford then asked a question on redirect: "Would the wound to the hip cause excruciating pain?"

"Yes, sir," Smith replied. Some would obviously think that the initial shotgun wound would constitute torture in and of itself.

The DA then called Dr. Steven Sims of Memphis, a physical anthropologist who briefly testified about the knife and axe marks on the victim's bones. Sims said the "chop marks" on the upper legs and arm were made by a heavy instrument with a wide "vee" like an axe would make. A small instrument made six fine-edged marks on the back of the victim's ribs, which would be compatible with the blade of a knife.

The forensic evidence tightened up a great deal with the testimony of TBI Nashville serologist Raymond DePriest, a specialist in blood testing. DePriest told the court that he had received eleven items for testing from Daniels, along with samples from the medical examiner. The axe, shovel, gravel and shoes taken from Ramsey were among those items.

DePriest testified that samples taken from the axe, shovel, shoes and gravel from Parrish Road all proved consistent with Brooks' Type A blood. Samples taken from the highway near Noles' home proved to be human blood, but could not be typed. No blood could be found on the shotgun, clothing, radio or knives taken from Harris' kitchen; of course, Harris testified that authorities had overlooked the knife used in the killing and had mistakenly taken others for testing, so that came as no surprise.

DePriest acknowledged to Weems that he had been given no sample of blood from Harris. He said if she had Type A, then her blood would also be consistent with the samples evaluated. The expert said Type A was the second most common type of blood, possessed by 37-percent of all people. Type O was most common at 46-percent, while B and AB were 13 and 3-percent respectively.

The blood matter might have been resolved completely by DNA tests, however, that was not to be. TBI DNA specialist Constance Howard said the samples received from Brooks' burned body were too poor in quality for an accurate determination. Every attempt to compare the specimen to the other samples had failed.

There was some comparison of the blood samples, however. She told Radford that she had matched the blood on the shovel to the blood on the shoes taken from Ramsey in a 1-in-52 probability when compared against other white humans. Such odds sound impressive, but broken down statistically it meant that perhaps seventy-five people in Huntingdon—and more than five hundred in the county—could have a similar consistency.

Weems inquired only if she had received Harris' sneakers for testing. She said that she had not.

TBI forensic firearms expert Steve Scott wrapped up the state's list of expert witnesses. Scott said he received the wadding and pellets taken from the two shotgun wounds. From those items, he determined that the shells used had been manufactured by Winchester and had been either 16 or 20-gauge. Five unused Winchester shotgun shells found inside a pair of shoes owned by Smothers proved to be 20-gauge with number 3 size shot; those shells were consistent with the rounds used to kill Brooks.

The state's final witness was Linda Brooks, the victim's mother. Although the pain was clearly etched upon her face, Mrs. Brooks, a nurse at Jackson-Madison County General Hospital, managed to keep her emotions in check during her brief stint upon the witness stand.

DA Radford had only one question and that concerned her late son's size. The medical examiner had not been able to give a size or weight because of the condition of the body and, obviously, Radford wanted that in the record and before the jury. It would also indicate that the victim was not a huge person who might have posed some special threat to the trio of killers. The witness said her son was about 5'9" or 5'10" and weighed between 155 to 160 pounds.

Defense attorney Weems had only one question for the woman as well. He asked if her son had a "high-pitched voice." The witness said he had a normal voice, but that it could become high-pitched while he was playing basketball.

With the state's case concluded it was time for the defense to make the rote motions to dismiss. Weems did so, moving that on count one, first-degree murder, the judge direct a verdict of acquittal, as there was no proof of premeditation or a deliberate killing. Radford countered that the trio had decided to stop someone and understood that it might be necessary to kill the person hijacked, which formed the required premeditation.

However, Radford said the state would like to dismiss that count and proceed only on count two of the indictment, which was felony murder in the perpetration of another felony—the charge that can draw the death penalty. Judge Guinn granted that motion.

Weems requested a continuance until the following day, stating he would be able to present all his case then. He said the first witness would take a considerable time and that there were three witnesses total. Radford had no objection to the continuance.

"I would like to get the case to the jury tomorrow," said Guinn in granting the motion for continuance. The judge then

74

instructed the jury that the count alleging first-degree murder had been dismissed and the remaining charge was murder during the commission of a felony.

On Wednesday morning before Harris took the stand, Weems informed the court that he had withdrawn the notice of intent to use an insanity plea. Psychological experts from Bolivar had been subpoenaed on Harris' behalf; their testimony would be saved for the sentencing hearing should Harris be found guilty, however. At that point, there seemed to be little doubt in the mind of anyone who had witnessed the trial thus far that the witnesses would indeed be testifying.

Weeping and shivering as she had throughout most of the proceeding, Deion Harris mounted the witness stand. Clad in a two-piece green suit and with a matching ribbon adorning her blonde hair, she more resembled a sweet young girl who had just lost her puppy than a cold-blooded murderer who would kiss a dead man's heart fresh from his bloody chest. Under Weems' gentle prodding, the woman detailed a number of experiences from her past life, most of them bad.

It was a tale heard far too often in modern America: a story of youthful involvement with drugs and alcohol, teenage pregnancy, broken relationships, an elusive search for something always just beyond the grasp. A marriage too young and two children, ages four and five, and a divorce in 1992. Then there was Smothers, whom Harris said she had met while attending Huntingdon High—somewhat later than Smothers had claimed.

"It wasn't a good relationship. I was scared of him," she told Weems. "The only reason I stayed with him was he supplied me with drugs and alcohol. I was addicted to them."

Radford would later attack her addiction claim, noting that she had experienced no withdrawal symptoms following her arrest. A psychologist alleged that she might have had a psychological addiction that did not manifest itself in physical symptoms.

Harris claimed that the only time she had sexual relations with Smothers was when she was high. Once, he began cutting his chest with a knife while they were having sex and threatened to cut her too. It was one of the reasons she feared him.

The woman went through much of the same testimony offered earlier by Smothers, but with a different take on many things. She related how Ramsey had been invited over and, after the phone run-in with Hampton, it was decided he would go with them to the fight. She said Smothers told Ramsey to go get his gun—what was never explained was how, if Smothers had only met the man a short time before, he even knew Ramsey owned a gun.

According to Harris, when she had gone by her ex in-laws to drop off the kids, her former husband, Jim Harris, had gotten into a disagreement with Smothers because he (Harris) had wanted her to stay there as well. She said that Smothers had insisted that she accompany him and Ramsey and he forcibly put her in the truck. Harris said she well knew the way to Hampton's house, but purposefully did not tell Smothers that evening.

"I told him I couldn't find it," she said. "I didn't want nothing to happen."

She acknowledged that Smothers told her she was "young and pretty" and could get someone to stop after the truck broke, but denied there was any previous discussion about robbing or killing anyone. She also said she did not know Smothers had the shotgun outside the truck.

"I thought I was just getting us a ride," she sobbed. Harris admitted screaming at Brooks after he was stopped and flung to the ground, but had what she thought was a good reason to do so.

"I told him to be quiet so he wouldn't kill him," she cried. "I hit him in the back, I didn't hit him in the head. I was telling him to be quiet so Walter wouldn't shoot him." That did not jibe with Noles' testimony of what was heard that night, nor with Smothers' previous testimony.

Smothers got upset because he thought the boy had lied to him about how much money he had on him. She said Brooks said he had $10 when asked, but Smothers found $13 when he took the man's wallet. That angered him.

She admitted covering the victim in the bed with the shotgun at one point.

"What would you have done if Dennis Brooks had jumped out of the truck?" Weems asked.

"I'd let him go," she replied.

Harris said she had handed the gun back to Smothers and had turned around in the seat to face forward when she heard it discharge and heard the wounded man scream. Smothers told her he had slipped and fallen and the gun had gone off accidentally, and that he had not meant to shoot Brooks.

"The boy screamed when the shot went off," she said. Smothers told him to lie down and shut up, "loud, like he was excited."

Harris said she believed Smothers when she heard him tell Brooks that they were going to take him to the hospital. As they approached the lights of Hollow Rock a short time later, she heard the gun blast once more and turned, horrified, to see what had happened.

"Walter said, 'I blew his fucking brains out,'" she sobbed. She and Ramsey then exchanged glances and it was like "we were both in shock."

According to the witness, once back at the house there was no discussion about what to do with the body. Smothers simply took over and issued orders, directing Ramsey to get the axe and shovel and her to obtain the butcher knife.

"I was scared he would kill me too," she said. "He acted like he knew what he was doing, like he had done this before."

Once at Haunted Bridge, Smothers began the mutilation. She said he chopped off one leg and then handed the axe to Ramsey and ordered him to chop the other. She said Smothers was the one who took the knife and began stabbing the victim.

"He was stabbing him and talking to him like he was still alive." During this entire portion of testimony, the Brooks family, including grandparents, sat in the courtroom sobbing quietly. It was a tragic thing to behold, such anguish caused by the trio of miscreants.

Harris said that she had stabbed Brooks once in the stomach only because Smothers had made her. It was also Smothers' idea to remove the victim's heart.

"He handed it to me and told me to drink the blood," she wept. "I put it to my lips but I didn't drink it." She then dropped the organ onto the gravel road, which angered Smothers because she "got it dirty." He picked it up and drank blood from it, then passed it to Ramsey and told him to drink.

The medical examiner had testified that the heart, which had been located in the victim's abdominal cavity, had a strange mark on the backside. The mark could have been made by suction from someone's mouth, he opined, however, it could have been made in some other manner as well.

Harris then related how they had gone back to the house for gasoline to burn the truck and body. She said she went along with it because she feared Smothers would kill her or her children. "He said in two days this was going to happen again," she sobbed.

The men took the radio from the truck before burning it. Smothers had taken three coins off the victim; one, a Grover Cleveland coin given to him by his grandfather. He had also taken Brooks' ball cap and sunglasses.

"Walter gave them to me the next day," she said of the "gifts."

The woman acknowledged that she had told Daniels what happened when he and the other officers came to her house, as the agent had told her, "I wasn't gonna be arrested as long as I told the truth." She knew the radio and coins were inside the house when she gave permission to search, but said she did not know the bloody axe and shovel were on the grounds.

As for the drinking at the tavern on the evening following the slaughter, Smothers had wanted to go. "But I wanted to go, too," she admitted.

The district attorney then got his shot at the woman in cross-examination and he began with her contention that Smothers had cut himself during sex. He wondered why there had been no previous mention of such an action and, if it had happened, why her attorney had not had the man expose his chest during his testimony.

"Could I suggest to you that was because (the scars) weren't there?" Harris had no answer to that.

Radford then questioned her previous relationship with Hampton and why nothing had been said before about a "knot on her head" that Hampton allegedly put there.

"You wanted Smothers to get Mr. Hampton, didn't you?"

"*I* wanted to get him," she replied.

"He (Hampton) wasn't worth killing, was he?"

"No."

The DA suggested that the only reason Harris did not take Smothers and Ramsey to Hampton's house was because the truck was about to quit, not because she was concerned for his safety. She denied that, stating, "No, I could have taken them straight to it."

She said she did not know what was going to happen when she stopped Brooks' vehicle.

"He *did* stop, didn't he, and that was a mistake, wasn't it?" Radford said.

"Yes," she replied in a small voice.

She admitted striking Brooks, but only because Smothers told her to. She said she hit him on the back.

"Did he tell you to call him a motherfucker, or was that your idea?" Radford inquired.

"Mine," she answered.

"You just sort of ad-libbed that," Radford said sarcastically.

As for the events leading up to the shooting of Brooks, Harris admitted she had held the shotgun on the young man—as in most instances, only because Smothers had told her to do it.

"Did it surprise you that holding a shotgun on somebody, somebody might get shot?" Radford inquired in an incredulous tone.

"To tell the truth, I didn't know it was loaded," the witness replied.

"Did he plead, 'Don't kill me, please don't kill me?'"

"Yes," she sobbed.

"That's when you said, 'Shoot the motherfucker', didn't you?"

"No, I didn't say that."

The witness again said that the only reason she had stabbed the victim was because Smothers had told her to and she was afraid not to do it.

"If I told you to take the knife and stab your son or daughter would you do that?" Radford asked. She said she would not. The DA then suggested that she was not afraid of Smothers at all.

"That night I was," she answered.

The question of whether or not she and Smothers had prayed to Lucifer that night was then raised. She contended that Smothers had asked her to join him in a prayer to the devil, but she did not and he prayed alone. Harris denied that she had told cellmate that they had prayed to Lucifer on the night of the killing.

"Did you feel a presence of some kind?" asked the DA.

"I could feel *something*. It wasn't good."

"Didn't you tell her that you got a rush when you did that?"

"I said I felt something," Harris responded.

"Didn't you tell her Dennis Brooks was a sacrifice to Lucifer?" asked Radford.

"I did not."

Radford asked if Harris had told people that she had difficult time getting the smell off her. She admitted she had.

"Mrs. Harris, how did you get the smell *on* you?"

"By standing there, I guess."

"Have you convinced yourself that you haven't done anything wrong?"

"I know I did wrong."

"You know you're guilty, don't you?" Radford said. She nodded her head.

Under re-direct examination by West, Harris said she felt guilty for stopping the truck and for stabbing the victim after he was already dead, but said, "No, I don't feel like I'm guilty of first-degree murder."

During a break following Harris' testimony, Huntingdon attorney John Everett Williams (now a member of the Court of Criminal Appeals), who was appointed by the Brooks family as its representative, made an official comment to the reporter outside the courtroom: "The Brooks family believes Teresa Harris is a liar and an actress, and not a very good actress," said Williams.

With the testimony concluded and the defense holding further witnesses until a possible sentencing hearing, it was time for closing arguments before the jury. During his closing statement, Radford acknowledged that the state had given some consideration to Smothers with the plea deal.

"Did we cut him a deal, give him some slack? Maybe. The state takes the position that his testimony was crucial for you to know the truth."

Radford said the defense attorney, during his the cross-examination question of Linda Brooks, tried to imply that the scream heard was too high-pitched to have been made by the victim.

"Had Mrs. Brooks ever heard her son scream after he was shot in the side with a 20-gauge shotgun?" demanded Radford in an indignant tone.

The DA then turned his attention toward the defendant, pointing at her.

"Look at her over there with her defense counsel holding her hand. You might say, 'That little gal couldn't do something like that, she looks too sweet.'" He paused for a moment before continuing. "You will make the same mistake Dennis Brooks, Jr. made at about one o'clock in the morning. She's a mean, vicious, murdering woman!"

The DA pointed out that Harris and Smothers had been at Casey's tavern the night after the murder and she was "bopping around" a little more than usual, wearing the victim's ball cap.

"That's how much she thought of Dennis Brooks. She was at the bar having fun," he said.

Radford said he could not tell the jury that there was any evidence she pulled the trigger. "I can tell you there *is* evidence that she aimed the gun at him and that the gun went off and shot him."

Criminal responsibility was not complicated, the DA explained. When more than one person commits a crime and any one of them killed another, *all* of them were guilty by default.

"The state is not required to prove she pulled the trigger," said Radford, which drew an immediate objection from Weems, his third during closing arguments. The defense attorney was quickly overruled by Judge Guinn, as he had been on the prior two occasions.

The defense contended that the only evidence against the defendant came from the mouth of an admitted murderer, a man who acknowledged shooting a man under the chin with a shotgun. Weems said his client was guilty only of knowingly mistreating a corpse or unlawful disposal of a body—felonies that carried a one-to-six year range of imprisonment; crimes for which she was not charged. He also noted that the shotgun had to be reloaded and cocked before the second, final round was fired.

"Is Deion to be held criminally responsible for Walter Smothers reloading and pulling the trigger?" he asked the jury.

According to the defense attorney, Harris did not intend to commit any sort of criminal act that evening. He said she had been surprised when Smothers appeared with the shotgun after she flagged Brooks down. She testified that she would not have shot the man had he escaped from the truck bed while she held the weapon. He said there was no proof presented that she assisted Smothers in robbing, kidnapping or shooting Brooks.

The attorney noted some differences in Smothers' statements, saying in the first statement the man had claimed to have slipped and fallen, thus discharging the firearm by accident. In the more recent statement, he claimed he was trying to take the gun from Harris' hand when it discharged.

In his final closing statement to the jury—the "second bite of the apple" enjoyed by the state during trials—Radford said it had been proven Harris had taken part in the entire scenario. She had flagged down Brooks while the other two hid, she had struck and cursed him after he was dragged from the truck, and she had held the shotgun on him.

"If that's not proof to you, how can we prove it?" asked the DA in an incredulous tone.

Following a charge in the applicable law by Judge Guinn, the jury began deliberations at 4:30 p.m. The short time they were out before announcing a decision would not bode well for the defense.

During the brief deliberations, Radford told the media that the Brooks family had decided to spare Smothers' life for his testimony and they had put a lot of thought into the decision. Even if a death sentence had been secured, there would be fifteen years or more of appeals and there was also a possibility the conviction might be overturned on appeal. Radford said Daniels was undergoing chemotherapy and might not be available for any future trial a reversal would require.

"It was the proper thing to do under the circumstances, a wise thing to do," said the DA of the family's decision to go along with a plea deal. "I felt the testimony of the co-defendant was crucial to this case."

Dennis Brooks, Sr. also had some comments for the media during deliberations. Brooks cited a Bible precept: *There can be no justice without judgment.* "All we're looking for is justice," he said.

The father of the victim said that any of the defendants could have gotten the same deal Smothers opted to take.

"You have to face his life, he will find prison life like nothing he's ever experienced," he said. He said that Smothers needed to ask forgiveness for his deeds. When asked if he had forgiven the man who murdered his son, he replied in the affirmative.

"Yes, but it has nothing to do with justice. I can't be mean-hearted. This is not my judgment, it's the court's."

As for his dead son, Brooks lamented the fact that the family had not gotten to say goodbye to him as would be typical at a funeral. "My son was not present at his own funeral," he said. "We'll always love him, he'll not be forgotten."

During the time the jury was out, the court also accepted Smothers' guilty plea. Standing before the judge, Smothers, clad in a green short sleeve shirt and jeans and chains, admitted to the crimes.

"I sentence you to the Tennessee Department of Corrections for the rest of your natural life, without the possibility of parole," pronounced Judge Guinn, adding, "Take him away!"

Radford told the court that Smothers wished him to express his remorsefulness to the Brooks family.

Word reached the courtroom at 5:35 p.m. that the jury had arrived at a verdict. In most cases, quick resolution works against the defense. In the case just heard, and with the damning evidence presented by the state, it appeared highly unlikely that any juror could effectively argue "reasonable doubt" existed.

The defendant sat at the table trembling like someone on the verge of a major nervous breakdown, however, that was little more severe than her normal state of emotions throughout the entire experience.

The verdict announced was just as expected: guilty of felony murder. The jury was polled one by one and unanimously announced the same verdict. Muffled sobs came from the now convicted murderess as Judge Guinn set the sentencing hearing for the following morning and released the four jury alternates from service.

Teresa Deion Harris was about to find out if she was going to die in the electric chair or spend the rest of her life caged like an animal. Neither option could have sounded good to the quaking young woman, nor could the handholding and back patting by her defense attorneys have had much of a calming effect.

The sentencing hearing began Thursday morning. Weems kicked the day off by complaining that the prosecutor had not complied with an order that a bill of particulars concerning the aggravating factors be provided to the defense. Those would be the factors the state would rely upon to request the ultimate penalty. He asked that the aggravating factors be stricken from consideration because of the state's failure to provide them.

"It's simply not true," responded DA Radford. He said the order had been complied with on October 24, however, Weems saw it differently, arguing that the bill had addressed only the case and not the aggravating factors. Judge Guinn was having none of it.

"You have everything before you that you are entitled to have," Guinn told Weems.

That did not placate the defense attorney, who attempted to object again. Radford spoke up: "Maybe Mr. Weems can't read, Your Honor," he said, and then read from the bill of particulars previously submitted to the defense. Guinn overruled Weems, and in a manner that suggested he did not want to hear further on the matter.

Radford explained the aggravating factors to the jury during his opening comments. Those were the elements the state relied on to raise the offense to capital murder and bring the death penalty into play.

In the case at hand, one was that the crime was atrocious and cruel and inflicted more pain than was necessary to cause death. The second involved a murder committed for the purpose of avoiding arrest and prosecution for other felonies committed—robbery and kidnapping, for instance.

Of course, at that point the only thing the defense could do was to suggest things that might mitigate Harris' responsibility to some degree and cause the jury to show mercy on her. Possible elements were her young age, her history of drug and alcohol abuse, mental health problems, personality disorders—*anything* that might remove her a step from the cold-blooded nature of the abduction, murder and mutilation.

During his opening statement, Weems said that he and co-counsel West had come to know Harris during the eight months they had represented her.

"You as a jury know her only as a murderer. We will attempt to show you in a few hours what we have learned in eight months. She is more than a murderer; she is a person who deserves compassion."

Weems told the jury that they would hear from Harris' sister and from a psychologist. "We will attempt to show you how a person like Deion could become involved in such an act," he said, adding that he was not trying to reduce the significance of what had happened to Brooks Jr.

The state's first witness at the sentencing was Brooks Sr., who no doubt surprised many observers during his time on the stand. After detailing all the facts about his family as previously noted, he said he and his family had decided that they did not want another family to feel the pain they had felt at the loss of a child. The witness said he had seen the aging that had taken place on the faces of his wife, his parents and his children during their terrible ordeal.

Radford asked if he was asking the jury to spare Harris' life and sentence her to life imprisonment without the possibility of parole.

"Yes sir, I am. I feel justice would be served if someone who committed this crime never walked free again," Brooks said emotionally.

That would not be the case in the later trial of Ramsey, as there were no appeals to spare him and the state again went after the death penalty in a serious way. Some might have found that odd because, on a scale of actual responsibility, Ramsey might have had a degree or two less to do with the actions that precipitated the murder than the other two.

Brooks' testimony had a dramatic effect upon some members of the jury. The jury foreman and two women on the panel brushed tears from their eyes as he spoke. To a courtroom observer, it seemed highly unlikely that the jury would go against the wishes of the grieving father, and yet the emotion shown indicated that feelings might run deep enough that such was possible. Weems and West surely breathed a small sigh of relief, as their primary purpose at the point in the trial was to keep their client off Death Row and hope for some relief on appeal.

Weems elected not to cross-examine the state's sole witnesses. Nothing could be gained by asking the emotional man about other facets of the case or family situation, other than perhaps to provoke some response that might further inflame the jury. Moreover, Brooks had already given the defense a powerful gift with his appeal to spare Harris' life.

Instead, the defense attorney called Harris' sister, Denise Taylor, to the stand. Taylor detailed some of the family's background and how the case had affected her sister. She related how their mother had suffered from severe arthritis and was hospitalized on several occasions for joint replacements. Deion, who was a "mama's baby," had to stay with her grandmother at such times and had begun sneaking around and drinking at the age of 12.

"After she took her first drink, she wanted more," said Taylor, weeping.

The 1982 death of their grandmother in an auto accident seemed to drive Harris further over the edge. She wandered off into the world of drugs, using cocaine and morphine, shooting up dope. She was committed for drug treatment a couple of times without much success and made her first suicide attempt at the age of 14, ingesting a whole bottle of Tylenol. That had happened over a boyfriend problem. In 1994, while in high school, she got pregnant the first time but managed to complete her studies by use of a homebound program. She was still deep in the world of drugs and alcohol during that time.

"At night she would call me and say, 'Denise, please help me,'" the witness cried.

According to Taylor, Harris went from one relationship to another, always with men who treated her badly and supplied her with drugs and alcohol. She became pregnant again in 1988 and entered into a "very cruel marriage" with Jim Harris, Taylor contended. She said her sister stayed with the man because of drugs and alcohol, though they eventually divorced. There were other men afterward, including Hampton, whom Taylor said, "had a nasty mouth on him." She claimed Hampton injured her sister several times during the year she lived with him.

As for Smothers, Taylor said, that was another case where her sister took up with a man for the drugs he could provide.

"She didn't really know him. They were only together two weeks."

DA Radford attempted to put the very upset witness at ease before he began cross-examination.

"I'm not going to be mean to you, you can relax a little," he said gently. "I know your son, he's a fine young man."

The DA then asked about her siblings. Taylor said she had a brother, Lynn, who was 18. Deion was 23 and she was 28. She and her brother were doing well and neither of them used drugs. Their father drove a school bus and had a lawn mower repair shop. Other than for the defendant and her problems, things were going pretty well. The whole family had tried to help Harris.

"You haven't been able to do much with her, have you?" asked Radford.

"No sir."

"She's gone down the road that led to where she is now, hasn't she?"

"Yes sir."

That concluded Radford's examination. Weems then came back and asked another question: Was there something Taylor had not wanted to discuss? She responded affirmatively. She agreed to discuss it if no names were used. She then said that her sister was raped and sexually abused at the age of 12 and that her major problems began about that time.

That line of questioning was pursued no further by either side. In most cases, children who fall victim to continuing sexual abuse do so at the hands of family members or close family friends and the refusal to name names or discuss the matter in more depth no doubt caused many observers to draw that conclusion.

Weems then presented Dr. Phillip Morson, a doctor of osteopathy with two and a half years service at Western Mental Health Facility in Bolivar. The doctor explained that he was certified to examine persons for competency to stand trial. DA Radford later questioned the difference between an osteopath and a regular medical doctor. Morson said the osteopath took a more holistic approach to medicine and sometimes did manipulative work much like a chiropractor.

He told the court he had his first contact with Harris on January 15, after she entered on an emergency basis following a suicide attempt at the Carroll County jail the previous evening.

According to Morson, Harris was suffering from major depression with an accompanying psychosis, all worsened by posttraumatic stress disorder—the latter a condition identified in returning Vietnam War veterans and called "shell shock" in earlier wars. The doctor said he saw Harris twice a week for two months and treated her with a combination of drugs and individual therapy. Her condition was such that she had difficulty determining if an event was actually happening or not, and it was triggered by witnessing, or participating in, the murder.

"Actually, at times she felt the deceased was in the room with her and she was hearing his voice begging," said Morson.

"At times, I had to put my forehead against hers just to get her back into the room."

Morson said Harris wanted to die because of the crime and cried each time it was brought up, "twisting her hair and going off into another world." Her guilt feelings arose because she could not stop Smothers from doing what he had done, and there was also guilt for being with the man in the first place. On one occasion at the hospital, she broke a window glass and attempted to cut herself with it.

Morson explained that PTSD affected different people in different ways—even combat soldiers in similar situations. The more horrible the experience was, the greater the likelihood of more negative impact upon the victim, he said. As for Harris, she dreamed of the horrors she had witnessed and relived them in her mind.

Radford handed the man a document, apparently a suicide note.

"She said, 'I'm going to kill myself, I don't deserve to live for what I've done?'" asked the DA.

"Yes," said Morson.

The distinction between the words "what I've done" and *what I've seen* should have been very clear to everyone in the courtroom. That distinction seemed to blow a big hole in the idea that Harris was haunted by what she had *seen* happen, not necessarily what she had herself *done*.

Following a lengthy recess caused by the delayed arrival of a Nashville clinical psychologist, Weems put the defendant on the stand for one question: did she have anything she wished to say to the Brooks family?

"I'd like to say I'm truthfully sorry for what happened," Harris said tearfully. "I know it won't bring your son back."

Radford did not question Harris. Weems told Judge Guinn that his witness was somewhere between Nashville and the courthouse but, "the exact whereabouts I don't know." Judge Guinn said he would allow more time and called another recess. Dr. Gillian Blair showed up thirty-five minutes later.

The British-born clinical psychologist said she had examined Harris for eight hours in February and administered several tests. She had found Harris to be suffering from major depression, PTSD and chemical dependency. The defendant also had an underdeveloped personality and a personality disorder, and possessed a borderline intellect. She was very dependent upon others—especially men.

Weems wondered if Harris might comply if a man told her to take a heart and kiss it. Blair said that was most likely because she may well have been very frightened.

"But it's hard to know how she or anyone else would react in that situation," Blair added.

Radford suggested to the witness that Harris was feeling stress over the trauma she incurred when she participated in the murder of Brooks, not something that had happened in the past. Blair acknowledged that the PTSD developed *following* some stressful event, thus it had no bearing on what had transpired prior to the time Brooks was murdered. The psychologist opined that Harris likely functioned better intellectually at the age of 18 than she did on February 18, 1994, when she interviewed the woman—probably an accurate assessment of *anyone* who has overindulged in drugs and alcohol for many years. Blair said Harris could still have a drug dependency; the fact that she had not received treatment following her arrest did not necessarily mean she was not an addict.

"In other words, she'd like to get high if she got the chance," Radford quipped, adding that Harris had testified she had no drug withdrawal symptoms.

"I assume she would know," said Blair.

At the conclusion of the hearing and prior to the judge's charge to the jury, Weems again moved to strike the aggravating circumstances. The judge overruled that motion in no short order.

"The record is replete with evidence to the first aggravating circumstance, if indeed not the second," said Guinn.

In his closing comments, Radford defined Harris as the nexus of the murder.

"It all comes back to Deion, she is the central player in the whole plot," he told the jury. He noted that Ramsey was involved because of her actions and that the problem that day arose from her conflict with Hampton, an old boyfriend. She had been the one who stopped the truck driven by Brooks because, "they all played off her."

His voice quivering with emotion, the DA said that some events change the lives of people forever.

"On July 30, 1993, in a remote, desolate area of Carroll County, such an event happened and all of us realize the change," he said. "The jury must speak for the people you represent. The State of Tennessee submits to you that this is a proper and fitting case for the penalty of death."

Weems, who lost two objections during Radford's closing statement, waived his right to address the jury one final time. The judge then instructed the jury on what possible penalties they could return.

Those included death, the possibility of life without parole, or regular life, which would require twenty-five calendar years before eligibility for parole. The jury left the room at 2:11 p.m. and sent word twenty-nine minutes later that they had arrived at a verdict. That verdict was announced four minutes later.

Standing supported between her attorneys, Teresa Deion Harris heard Judge Guinn sentence her to the rest of her natural life in the state Department of Corrections. Members of her family wept quietly in the background as she was led away by guards to begin a lifetime behind walls and bars. She was transported back to the Carroll County jail where she was held until adequate space opened up in the state penal system.

Following the trial, Brooks family spokesman Williams said the Brooks family wished to convey its deepest appreciation to the citizens of Henry County and to the members of the jury, who had acted "in a courageous and just manner throughout the whole ordeal."


With two of the three cases resolved, the only action remaining was the case against Stacy Ramsey. Immediately following Harris' conviction in Henry County, co-counsel Matt

Maddox told the reporter that he would seek another change of venue because of the massive amount of publicity the case had generated there.

The change of venue was granted by Judge Guinn during hearing held Thursday, April 14. Guinn told attorneys that he would determine a new venue by the weekend. During conference call the following day with all the attorneys involved the judge set Montgomery County as the site of the trial, with the proceedings to be held in Clarksville, 62 miles from Paris by automobile.

The Maddox team was less successful in yet another attempt to have Judge Guinn recuse himself from hearing the case because of alleged prejudicial statements he had made. DI Maddox told the court that he would like to introduce evidence concerning the statements.

"Call your witnesses," said Guinn in his no-nonsense manner.

"I would call Your Honor as the first witness," said the somewhat flamboyant attorney, known for wearing his dark hair long in the back in a fashion that, with his skin tone and facial features, made him resemble a Native American.

The well-known defense attorney was something of contrarian. When smoking was banned inside the Carroll County courthouse, Maddox defied the order by lighting up on the second floor stairwell in the presence of Judge Logan and the dared he judge to do something about it. The judge let it be known that he was not going to be pressed on the issue and Maddox extinguished the smoke after a few puffs, apparently feeling he had made his point.

Judge Guinn seldom gave away any emotion with his facial expression, other than perhaps a brief hint of anger at some incompetence exhibited before him. If the incompetence was too severe, he could explode.

On one occasion, an assistant DA had attempted to offer video recording during a hearing. The tape was not wound to the proper spot and the DA was not at all familiar with the machinery or how to operate it. During several minutes of fumbling, Judge Guinn became almost apoplectic and chastise the red-faced prosecutor to no end.

Maddox's attempt to put him on the witness stand resulted in the jurist's face turning into a mask of pure indignation and it was instantly obvious that he would not comply.

"No, you are *not* going to call me!" Guinn thundered emphatically.

Undeterred, the defense attorney then took a different tack and attempted to call Assistant DA Cahill, whom he had subpoenaed. DA Radford was on his feet immediately objecting to that move, noting that Cahill was prohibited by law from expressing any opinion. Cahill was not ordered to the stand.

"Your Honor has made statements concerning the reliability of witness Alvin Daniels," Maddox told Guinn. The attorney also alleged that Guinn had engaged in "improper" *ex parte* (private) conversations with the DA about Harris and some of those comments had made their way into the newspapers. He said Guinn should recuse himself, not because he was prejudiced, but to avoid any *appearance* of impropriety.

The judge responded that he had *ex parte* conversations with all the attorneys involved, "including you," but that none of them were improper.

"I can't control what the newspapers report, whether it is correct or not," Guinn told Maddox. "If you'd like to know if I'd like to get off this case, I'd love to get off." However, he added that duty required he follow the case to its conclusion and that what he had, or had not, said was in the court record.

Guinn seemed to be advising the attorney that if he thought he could use the record to get a reversal for his client, go for it.

Maddox had better luck with a motion requesting the transcript of Harris' trial. Guinn ordered that the transcript, minus the testimony of three minor witnesses whose testimony had nothing to do with Ramsey, be supplied as soon as possible. He shot down a motion to delay the May 9 start of Ramsey's trial, which had been requested to gain additional time to review the Harris transcript, however, stating that Maddox was trying to "shotgun this whole thing" by making a number of unnecessary last minute requests.

"I'm taking issue with you; you should have anticipated this," said Guinn. Maddox countered that he and his partner were not present during the Harris trial and had no idea as to who had testified to what.

"Maybe the government should have anticipated it," Maddox retorted. "We didn't hear it and we're totally in the dark."

The judge said he would order the document transcribed and into the hands of the defense by May 2, or sooner if possible. That would give Maddox a week or more to review the material before Ramsey's trial began.

Guinn denied a motion to suppress evidence about the mutilation of Brooks' body after his death, finding it admissible as he had in Harris' case.

Ramsey's trial in Clarksville started May 9 with jury selection as scheduled, just three days after Deion Harris left the county jail for the women's prison in Nashville to begin serving her natural life sentence. Harris was subpoenaed by the defense to testify on Ramsey's behalf in his bid to escape the fate she had befallen, however, defense attorneys got a rude surprise when they attempted to question her.

Smothers, of course, would testify for the prosecution as he had in the case just concluded, which was part of the deal he had made to spare his life.

According to a report published in *The Jackson Sun*, Brooks did not intend to make a plea for the jury to spare Ramsey's life, as he had in the case of Harris. He reportedly said that he had tried to avoid another trial and that the jury would be the final arbiter of Ramsey's fate.

Ramsey had the opportunity to accept a sentence of life without the possibility of parole, but he had refused to do so. While there was a possibility the jury might award the death sentence were he found guilty—and it seemed likely he would be found guilty—there was also the possibility that he might receive a regular life sentence, which would make parole possible after service of twenty-five calendar years. Ramsey was gambling with his very life, but perhaps death was preferable to being forever caged.

Jury selection finally concluded well into the day on Tuesday and the state began putting on the first of its 18 evidentiary witnesses. Agent Daniels, very near the end of his life at that point, was first on and told essentially the same story he had told during Harris' trial. Dill, the Subway manager, also was on the stand briefly Tuesday and concluded testimony for that first day.

Wednesday kicked off with one of the twelve jurors being called before the bench and dismissed from service, with the judge appointing an alternate to take her seat. Judge Guinn explained only that a "family situation" involving a child had arisen, which required the juror's presence at home.

Bunn was the first state witness called Wednesday and he again related all the details of Noles' early morning call about voices, screams and a shot on the roadway near his Highway 114 home. He detailed how evidence had been taken from the road and bagged and how Ramsey's broken down truck had been discovered. He again told of finding the burning truck and how he had not known for certain what he was seeing when he looked inside the burned vehicle: "I didn't know if it was a human or a dog," he told Radford, adding that he could see what looked like bones around a rib cage.

Former CCSO Deputy Jason Fields—one of the officers suspended in the prank call hoax at the jail and an employee of the McKenzie Police Department since February 27—related how he had been the first officer to arrive on the scene when the burning truck was found. Fields had testified briefly in Harris' case, but not to any matters concerning the murder. In that case, he told how he had been dispatched to Casey's tavern to retrieve and deliver a pocketbook Deion Harris had left there the evening she and Smothers partied on the night following Brooks' murder.

Fields said he was patrolling on Highway 77 when he received a call about the burning truck and proceeded to the location, about seven miles away. A rural fire department had extinguished the fire by then. Fields secured the area and got names of all the firefighters involved. He told Radford that he later picked up Ramsey, who was a neighbor of his. He said he and another deputy went to the man's trailer in the early morning hours and found him on the couch. He informed Ramsey that the TBI wanted to talk to him. Ramsey said he did not know where his shoes were and thought they might be out front.

"I saw a pair of high-tops there and told him to put them on," Fields told Radford. Certainly, at that moment Fields had no inkling of the significance of those bloodstained shoes, as they would break the case wide open sometime later that morning when Daniels interviewed Ramsey.

Ramsey certainly knew where the shoes came from and no doubt wanted to wear another pair when questioned by the TBI. Having thought to attempt to get another pair so quickly after being rudely awakened from a drunken slumber might indicate that the man was somewhat sharper than the borderline mentality depicted by psychologist Auble.

Radford asked if Ramsey was drunk or sober and Fields said he was, "somewhere in between. He would have been DUI."

That was not a very telling statement, considering the fact that three beers would probably put a slender man Ramsey's size above the legal limit, although it would probably not result in an overtly drunk person. According to previous testimony, the man was so drunk that he could not be questioned until he sobered up later that morning.

While Ramsey was not under arrest at that time, Fields said he handcuffed the man "for both our safety."

Matt Maddox wanted to know who was with Fields when he went to Ramsey's home. The officer said that a reserve deputy, Jim Grant, was riding with him. Deputy Andy Dickson was in a separate car and he was the one who hauled Ramsey to the jail complex.

Fields said he yelled, "Stacy, sheriff's office, come to the door!" and Ramsey opened the door. He agreed to go along with the officers and caused no problem, cooperating fully.

Keith Noles, whose early morning phone call to the sheriff's office was the genesis of law enforcement's entry into the case, again told his story. He related how he and his wife had woken on the front porch to the sounds coming from the highway some 70-to-100 feet away. They heard yelling, cursing, a gunshot and a scream. Noles acknowledged to Maddox that he could not distinctly hear much of what was said, though some parts were fairly clear.

As in the Harris case, Walter Smothers proved to be the state's ace in the hole. Dressed in blue prison denims and with his ankles chained, Smothers took the stand Wednesday morning.

"Why are you in penitentiary clothes?" inquired DA Radford.

"For murdering Dennis Brooks, Jr.," Smothers replied matter-of-factly. He said he had agreed to a life without parole term in exchange for his testimony and that he had promised to tell the truth.

Smothers testified the same as he had during Harris' trial, with a few differences or additions. Previously, it was said that Ramsey came to Harris' house after Harris sent her young son over to invite him to come "smoke a joint" with her and Smothers. This time, Smothers said Ramsey did not immediately come following that initial invitation, but did after Harris herself went to get him. Prior to that, Harris had gone to a doctor and gotten a prescription for Valium to go along with the Budweisers they had started drinking around noon.

He again detailed the problems with Harris' former boyfriend, Hampton, that day, but came up with another motive for the trio finding the man.

"She wanted us to hold him down while she did to him what he did to her once before," said Smothers. Hampton had admitted that he and the woman had several altercations and claimed that she had once bitten his nose.

There was also some confusion about the appearance of the shotgun this time around. Smothers said he did not know when the shotgun came into the picture, though later acknowledged that he knew the shotgun was present when they left Harris' house that evening.

"When I seen the shotgun I took possession of it," he told Radford.

Ramsey had always contended that the shotgun was behind the seat of his pickup, while the prosecution alleged that he had taken it from his home especially for the mission to seek out Hampton. There seemed to be little doubt that it was Smothers who was carrying the shotgun when he and Ramsey emerged from hiding behind the broken pickup after Harris conned

Brooks into stopping. He had threatened Brooks and had handed the gun to Harris at one point just prior to the first shot.

"I pointed the shotgun at him and told him to get out," said Smothers. The victim complied and was then thrown to the ground by Ramsey. Harris then "slapped" the victim several times and then cursed him—in previous testimony, it was said that she had "struck" him in a manner that implied fists were used.

Smothers related the accidental discharge of the weapon as he attempted to take the gun back from Harris and the wounded man's cries. He told the court of firing the final round into the man's head to silence him, and about the "voices" he had heard directing him to do that.

"The voice inside your head that said shoot him, was that the devil?" DD Maddox later asked.

"I don't know what it was," Smothers replied, acknowledging that he had worshipped the devil only "a time or two."

This time around, Smothers gave ease of disposal as reason the body was chopped up; it was too late at that point to bury Brooks and he believed that chopping the body into pieces would make it easier to burn.

During cross-examination, Maddox asked if Smothers participated in the ritual of putting the excised heart to his lips.

"Yes, I did," he replied.

Maddox then produced a written interview that one of his investigators had conducted with Smothers. He noted that Smothers told the interviewer that Ramsey did not have a lot to say during the entire episode and that, after the initial accidental wounding of Brooks, Harris was responsible for about 90 percent of what occurred.

"Did you say that to her (the interviewer)," inquired Maddox.

"Yes, I did."

"Is it true?"

"Yes."

"You say Stacy was just there?"

"Yes."

"Is Stacy Ramsey very bright?"

"In my opinion, no."

Radford then countered by asking Smothers if Harris had told Ramsey to throw Brooks down, steal his radio, drive his truck or get the shotgun.

"She said we'd need one (shotgun)," Smothers replied, adding that Harris had not told Ramsey to do any of the other things.

TBI agent Steve Champine later testified that he had seen the shotgun propped in a corner at Ramsey's home when they went there to search for the deer hide Ramsey had claimed as an excuse for the blood on his shoes, but had thought nothing unusual about it at the time. In the locale in question, one could enter many homes and find shotguns propped in corners. However, when he arrested Ramsey about two hours later, Champine took the shotgun into his custody.

State medical examiner Smith testified once again, perhaps in somewhat more gruesome detail than in the earlier trial. Smith said that 66 pounds of remains were recovered, although the victim weighed close to 160 pounds at the time of his death. Certainly, the Brooks family was very emotional during Smith's testimony, no doubt remembering their son lying in Hampton Cemetery south of Huntingdon and the heartless animals that put him there.

Smith had initially said that the second wound to Brooks would have rendered him "unconscious and immovable." This time, he said the shotgun wound to the brain and spinal cord would have resulted in immediate death. Smith said he could tell that the body was burned after the chopping injuries by the burned condition of the exposed bone ends.

Sims, the forensic anthropologist, added his findings to the condition of the body. He told the court that the amputations were made high on the thighs with a coarse blade object like an axe or machete. There were fine cuts on the inside rib cage at the victim's back, which indicated that a blade had gone all the way through the body from front to back; in short, that the victim had been powerfully stabbed a number of times.

Former boyfriend Hampton, who Radford later (during closing arguments) said was "lucky to be alive," told his side of the story again, with one new comment not made during the Harris trial. He said that when he decided not to pay Harris $50 for the coat as originally proposed and called back, Smothers would not let him speak to Harris.

"I told him to tell her she could take the coat and shove it up her ass," the witness told Maddox.

The state's final witness was the grieving father, Dennis Sr. Struggling to keep his emotions in check, the man again related how he had moved his family from Memphis to Carroll County about a decade earlier to escape the high crime rate in the Bluff City; the irony of that could have been lost on only the most dense individual. He detailed how his son had failed to show up at noon to close the deal on the pickup and the search he made himself. And then, sobbing, he told how two of his son's friends had come to his home at midnight to tell him what they had heard on a police scanner about his son being found. He then called the sheriff's department.

"They (authorities) sort of put me off before," he wept. "I insisted on an answer." He then learned the awful truth that a body had been found and it was most likely his missing boy.

With the state concluding testimony at 4:00 p.m. Wednesday, the defense had time to call one witness prior to adjournment for the day. They elected to call Auble, the clinical psychologist.

The woman told DD Maddox that she had interviewed Ramsey on February 10 and again on May 5. She also administered a battery of tests designed to gauge his intelligence and truthfulness. He had done well on the latter and she believed he was telling her what he essentially believed to be true.

Investigators hired by the defense had interviewed sixteen of Ramsey's friends and relatives and that information had been passed along to Auble. DA Radford objected on the grounds of hearsay when Auble tried to introduce information collected in the interviews, however, Judge Guinn allowed it in, though he ruled it was subject to cross-examination.

According to the investigation, Ramsey's IQ had not changed much over the years. It was rated at 80 when he was 10 years old. Another test administered at 16 years of age placed it at 72. He had always performed below grade level in school and had extremely low language skills, Auble said.

She described the defendant as very immature and dependent and on the far end of the passive spectrum. He lacked social skills and had trouble interfacing with others; one former girlfriend told investigators that the man simply walked away from personal confrontations.

Some of that could probably be attributed to the fact that his mother had died in an auto accident when he was two, Auble speculated. His older sister had become very protective of him, while his father had been very demanding, teaching him to be a "people-pleaser," said Auble. She said he had also been placed under pressure by a grandfather while growing up in North Carolina.

It was Auble's opinion that Ramsey had been very frightened of Smothers on the night of the murder and remained frightened of him to that day.

"Stacy is in fear for his life," she told the court. "He remains frightened of him to the point he's afraid to be alone in a room with him."

As for Ramsey's memory of what happened on the night Brooks was killed, Auble said he had lapses. She believed the lapses were genuine and not contrived.

On cross-examination, Radford inquired as to who had hired her. She said the defense had. She acknowledged that she often worked with defense attorneys, but did not always testify for them.

"My job is to find out what Stacy is like as a human being. It's the lawyers' job to defend him," she told Radford.

Radford then suggested that the investigators had a specific result in mind when they made their inquiries. Auble countered that their job was to learn the truth. The DA also pointed out that Ramsey graduated fifty-eighth in a class of one hundred. Auble countered that she had no knowledge of the quality of the school, thus could not assess that standing in the class.

The DA wondered why Ramsey would have violently flung Brooks to the roadway if he was so passive and nonviolent. Auble suggested that might have been an attempt to keep Smothers from shooting him (Brooks).

"Do you want the jury to rely upon that, Ms. Auble?" asked Radford.

"I think he was scared to death. I don't think it's in him to stand up to Walter . . . he *should have*, I'm not arguing with you about that."

First thing Thursday morning, Maddox called Deion Harris to the stand as his first witness. Harris' attorney, Shipp Weems, was in the courtroom and addressed Judge Guinn.

"My understanding from talking to Ms. Harris yesterday is that she doesn't intend to testify," Weems told the judge. Guinn commented that a contempt citation and ten days in jail was not likely to concern her a great deal.

"We're entitled to put her on in the presence of the jury and if she won't talk, they have a right to know it," said DD Maddox. The judge then ordered Harris brought in and placed on the witness stand. Maddox asked her name.

"I'm sorry, I can't answer any of your questions," Harris replied.

The defense attorney asked if she could not at least tell her name and she did so. When he inquired why she would not answer his questions, she responded, "Because I don't want to."

Judge Guinn then instructed her in her obligation to testify.

"Do you refuse to testify?" Guinn asked.

"Yes sir, I do. I don't have to," she replied, somewhat cockily.

"Who told you that?"

"My lawyer," she answered.

Radford noted that the woman had testified at her own trial. He then began to ask her a series of leading questions about the shotgun and assaulting Brooks, framed so that the jury could derive a great deal of information from the unanswered questions. Harris did not respond and Judge Guinn finally pulled the plug on the DA's backdoor attempt to impart information to the jury.

"General, you've gone about as far with that as you can go," the judge told Radford. He then ordered Harris taken back into the custody of prison guards and transported back to the penitentiary, before addressing the jury as to why nothing was done to punish her for failure to testify.

"There is, quite frankly, nothing else I can do to her," said the judge—probably an understatement, considering that she already faced spending the rest of her life behind bars. Guinn did order that a copy of the transcript of her refusal to testify be entered into her prison record for whatever affect that might have on her situation at some future point.

With the courtroom theatrics of Harris' refusal to testify finished, Maddox then placed his client on the stand. The first question dealt with whether or not Ramsey was frightened of Smothers and Harris. The man said he was scared of Smothers, but "not really" scared of Harris.

"Two or three years ago, we dated a couple of times," he said. Later, under cross-examination, Ramsey would admit that he had been sexually intimate with Harris on more than one occasion.

The defendant told the court that he had been working on his truck that day when Harris sent her son, a boy about four or five, over to ask him to come smoke marijuana. The boy's message had been, "Deion wants you to come over and smoke a joint," he said, adding that "Deion" is what the child called his mother. He did not go at that point, but did later when Harris showed up and told him they were partying. It was about dark, around 8:15 p.m., when Ramsey crossed the Rubicon called Dillahunty Road and thus changed his life forever.

Ramsey said they drank beer and smoked dope. Around 9:30 came a phone call from Hampton, with whom Smothers argued.

"He wasn't really angry," said Ramsey of Smothers' phone conversation. "He acted like he was getting a kick out of arguing over the phone." There was a lot of cursing going on at the time.

A little while later, they all piled into Deion's T-bird and drove to Paris. They bought whiskey and tequila at a liquor store on Mineral Wells and then headed to the Kroger where they picked up a 12-pack of Bud. Walter paid for everything. Then they went back to Harris' little wood frame home and continued drinking.

"They were getting pretty tipsy, but were not falling down drunk," Ramsey said of his cohorts.

Sometime about 11:30 p.m., Smothers decided he wanted to find Hampton and fight. They dropped the kids off at Harris' former mother-in-law's home and got gasoline. When Maddox asked what role Ramsey had intended to play in the intended combat, the man replied, "I guess an observer, I don't know." The shotgun was in the truck at that point, behind the seat.

The witness said they went in his truck so he could "leave when he got ready" and because he was the least drunk of the three and could drive better—his remark about "leaving when he got ready" was somewhat odd, because it implied he might leave them somewhere, not likely for a man who feared Smothers as he professed. They drove around for some time trying to locate Hampton's place, but never did and had started home when the truck broke down.

Ramsey's claim that all the booze was gone by the time the truck broke was at odds with the earlier testimony of Smothers, who said they continued to drink after the pickup failed. He also denied that there was ever any discussion of commandeering a vehicle or possibly killing the driver. There had been no hiding behind the truck either, he said. Ramsey said he was looking into the engine compartment and did not pay much attention when Brooks stopped, but he heard Smothers yell and saw that he had a gun pointed at the victim.

"Were you scared of (Smothers)?" asked Maddox.

"I wasn't going to argue with him," replied Ramsey.

Ramsey did not see or hear a number of things already testified to by Smothers. He did not throw Brooks to the ground nor did he hear Harris say anything or see her strike the man. He said he never saw Harris with the shotgun in her hands and he said that he heard both shots before he ever turned the truck around and headed back toward Hollow Rock.

"Smothers said, 'I didn't mean to shoot him the first time. He wouldn't shut up and I had to shoot him again,'" Ramsey testified.

104

Ramsey said that he did not look into the bed of the truck, but had a good idea that the man was dead. He claimed that Smothers later removed the dead man's shoes and tossed them to Ramsey, saying, "If they fit, you can have them." Smothers had testified that Ramsey took the shoes off Brooks' feet on Parrish Road before they chopped his legs off.

Ramsey denied that he had gotten any implements from the well house as Smothers had claimed. He said that once they got to Haunted Bridge, Smothers cut the dead man's clothing off with a butcher knife and then sliced off his penis, saying, "He won't be needing this anymore."

The witness said he could not recall anything about the body being stabbed or the heart being removed. He claimed not to have participated in the dismemberment. He had not tried to run because he was afraid Smothers would catch him, he told Maddox.

According to Ramsey, they drove back to Harris' house with the body in the truck bed and changed clothing before disposing of the body. He said he wore a pair of Harris' shorts. Gasoline was taken from the well house, but Ramsey said he had no idea they were going to burn the body. He claimed there was never any discussion of using his father's backhoe to bury both the truck and body, as Smothers had testified.

That later claim caused Radford to wonder how Smothers knew the machine had a flat tire, which Ramsey admitted was true. It seems obvious that the witness was being somewhat disingenuous in much of his testimony.

Another of Ramsey's claims was met with skepticism by the DA. The defendant said that when they arrived at the field where the truck and body were burned, Smothers stuck the man in through the driver's side and then ordered Ramsey to pull him in from the passenger side. He said he did so by grasping both the victim's arms. As Radford noted, that would have been impossible, as Brooks' right arm had been chopped off earlier at Haunted Bridge.

Another point of disagreement arose over what happened after they set the truck ablaze. Smothers had testified that they then returned to Harris' house and cleaned up and slept, arising the next day to go back to the scene of Ramsey's disabled pickup on Highway 114. But according to Ramsey, they left the field and drove straight to where his pickup sat alongside the road. They arrived back home around 4:00 or 4:30 a.m. and Ramsey said he talked to his sister and her boyfriend out by the driveway. He told her he had to get his truck and she told him he had to get to work in ten or fifteen minutes, he said.

Ramsey said Smothers made up the alibi story about a black man driving a large black four-door sedan giving them a ride home. Radford noted that it had been about six months since that statement was discussed in court and observed that Ramsey had "a good memory, better than mine."

Ramsey slipped up when he said that Smothers had accompanied him when he went to take the shotgun "back" to the trailer. Radford keyed in on the word "back," since it seemed to imply that Ramsey had made a special trip to get the gun before setting off that evening, instead of merely having it already in his pickup before any trouble arose. The DA noted that one had to take something "from" some place in order to take it "back" to that place.

"It was in the truck, that's just words that I use," said Ramsey.

"It was a slip-up. You did get it out of the house, didn't you?" asked Radford. Ramsey denied it.

Radford then questioned if Ramsey did not have a problem with Hampton himself, as the man had lived with Harris after she dated Ramsey. Ramsey said he had no problem with Hampton.

"Mr. Hampton's a lucky man that truck broke down, isn't he?" asked Radford.

"I didn't think anybody was going to get killed," replied Ramsey.

"What were you going to do, watch it like the Friday Night Fights?" the DA retorted. Radford then told Ramsey that Smothers said he went to the house to get the shotgun.

"Mr. Smothers said a lot of things," Ramsey retorted.

Ramsey claimed he knew nothing about coins or any items taken from Brooks. He even knew nothing about Brooks' tool pouch found in his shed; he suspected Smothers might have been trying to frame him with that item.

According to the witness, the shotgun was unloaded initially. The shells were in the truck's glove box and he assumed Smothers found them. He said he heard Brooks screaming and begging for his life after the first shot. He did not recall hearing anything about taking the injured man to the hospital.

Ramsey acknowledged that what he had done was wrong, but insisted that he had no choice. He said he was sorry. Radford asked if saying he was sorry made everything all right.

"No, it doesn't make it all right," he replied.

The defense then called CCSO head jailer Carvene Jamison, who testified only that Ramsey had been cooperative while housed in the county jail. Jamison, in fact, had incurred some problems of his own concerning the situation when he was suspended for five days without pay that previous September for allowing male prisoners to mingle with Deion Harris.

DA Radford had announced on October 5, 1993, that he was calling for an investigation by the TBI into the operations at the sheriff's department and the county jail. That followed closely on the heels of the September 30 arrest of Sheriff Brandon in Paris on DUI charges, following a collision at an intersection. In his call for an investigation, Radford said there had been many complaints of lax security, drug use and sexual improprieties at the jail.

Sheriff Brandon was convicted of DUI following a jury trial in Henry County March 24. He was fined $500 and sentenced to two days in jail—the same penalty anyone would receive for a first-offense DUI; however, the jury elected to double the minimum $250 fine.

After the TBI investigation began and polygraphs were administered to personnel, jailer and sometimes-road deputy Skip Tucker was fired October 13. Jailer Mitchell Alexander resigned after being informed that he was being investigated for official misconduct.

The probe into county law enforcement ended Friday, April 22, with information  submitted to the grand jury for possible action. The grand jury gave the department a clean bill of health

May 2, but noted problems with inadequate staff and no liability insurance.

Rick Beckman, one of Ramsey's co-workers, next took the stand. Beckman was at Ramsey's house when Smothers and Harris came over later on the day of the killing. Ramsey had earlier said that Smothers made a comment that might have been a veiled threat. He told Ramsey's sister that she should be careful of her little girl because there was a "killer running around in the woods." Ramsey said that at the time, he figured Smothers might have told Beckman what had happened.

Beckman told Maddox that both Smothers and Harris were very intoxicated when they came to Ramsey's trailer. He said he had not thought much about Smothers' comment until he heard the three were arrested for the murder of Brooks. Smothers had the little girl sitting on his knee when he made the comment about the killer running loose in the woods and the need for caution.

That testimony undoubtedly made some wonder if perhaps the child might have been the next victim, come the time when the moon turned full and another victim had to go.

With the defense rested, DA Radford called Dr. Bernard Hudson of Carey Counseling Center to rebut Auble's testimony. Hudson said that he had spent one hour with Ramsey and an additional half an hour evaluating documents and he found no signs of mental illness or disease. Hudson also found the man capable of standing trial. The doctor had administered a reading test to Ramsey, using an advertisement from the cover of a phone book, and determined his reading level was junior high to early high school.

When asked by Maddox why he had not administered an IQ test, Hudson replied, "I am a child and adolescent psychiatrist. I don't have to. With my training and experience, I can guess someone's IQ within a couple of points."

When Maddox later said he did not know what Hudson could have perceived from an hour and a half of effort that did not involve any testing, the doctor became somewhat testy himself.

"That's exactly right, Mr. Maddox, you *don't* know. I can do quite a lot," Hudson retorted sarcastically.

Maddox also could not find much value in using a telephone book to perform a reading test. Hudson could not provide specifics on many of the details of his tests—it seemed the expert had failed to bring any of his notes concerning Ramsey to court with him.

Maddox rebutted Dr. Hudson by again calling his own expert, Auble, in what appeared to be a "gunfight of the experts." She once again testified that she had found Ramsey suffered from dependent personality disorder and pooh-poohed the notion that anyone could determine an IQ without proper testing.

"Is reading the back of a phone book a standard reading test?" asked Maddox.

"Not to my knowledge," Auble replied with something of a smirk. She did agree with the psychiatrist that Ramsey did not meet the criteria to support an insanity defense, however.

During closing arguments, Radford cautioned the jury about Ramsey's "selective amnesia."

"Don't try to make sense out of this, because there *is no sense* to it," he said of the killing. During another point in the summation, he mentioned one witness presented by the prosecution, a fellow who was not too well equipped mentally.

"Old So-And-So is a lot like us over in Carroll County, he is no Einstein," Radford said. "He's not smart enough to be a doctor or lawyer, but he's honest."

Maddox did not gloss over the gravity of his client's actions in closing arguments.

"I have to tell you from the beginning, Stacy Ramsey did some horrible things," he said to the jury. Maddox continued to note that it was "degree of guilt" that should be considered, in light of the man's fear of Smothers and his diminished mental capacity. Smothers was the "dominant person at the scene of the crime," and Harris he termed "the general of the army." Smothers was her "lieutenant" and Ramsey was but a poor foot soldier, caught up in the machinations of power beyond his ability to cope, hampered by mental defect and fear.

"You should consider that when determining the degree o crime you're going to find him guilty of," said Maddox. "That' what we implore you to do."

It was an odd moment in a trial, hearing an attorne acknowledge that his client would be found guilty of something Nevertheless, it was an unavoidable conclusion, in light of th testimony offered, even that of the defendant himself.

In his final closing, Radford resorted to a Jack Londo quote favored among prosecutors: "He who runs with the pac shares in the kill." The DA scoffed at the idea that Ramsey' childhood and family had caused him to have a mental defec that led him to take part in the grisly murder.

"He didn't kill (Dennis Brooks, Jr.) because he didn't get little red wagon when he was five years old," Radford thundered "They come in here and malign his father, blame it on hi granddaddy!"

Following Guinn's charge, the case went to the eight-mar four-woman jury at 4:10 p.m. Thursday. At 5:30, Guinn calle the jury back in and concluded deliberations for the day. The were back at it at shortly after nine o'clock Friday morning an arrived at a guilty verdict forty minutes later. Ramsey showed n emotion when the verdict was announced.

As had Harris, Stacy Ramsey faced three possibl outcomes from the finding of guilty of first-degree murde death, life without parole or life with the possibility of freedor after twenty-five years service. In his opening statement to th jury during the sentencing hearing that began moments after th mid-morning verdict, Radford made clear the state's intentions.

"I, on behalf of the people of Carroll County and the peopl I represent, will be asking for death," he told jurors.

Matthew Maddox said there were several mitigating factor to consider in his client's case that would allow jurors to mak the correct decision.

The prosecution's lone witness was Brooks Sr. The tru horror of what the trio had done that deadly night came to bea when one observed the large and powerful man reduced t emotional wreckage by the loss of his beloved son. His voic shaking with emotion, he again detailed his family life and tha of his son, whom he said had "a bright future" stretching before him until he encountered the three miscreants on Highway 114.

"To kill someone like that with no motive, no reason," he sobbed. "It's very hard to live with. I love my children more than I love life itself." The manner of his son's death made it more difficult—it was like something you would read about happening in another part of the world.

"I never imagined when we went looking for him that day what the outcome would be," he concluded.

The state rested its case with that testimony and it was time for the defense to have a go at swaying the jury away from the death sentence. Maddox first called Ramsey's father, James. James Ramsey described his son as an ordinary young man who grew up in North Carolina and moved to Tennessee in 1987.

"I tried to raise him like I was raised myself, to work and have something," James Ramsey told Maddox. "Stacy probably would have done better if he'd had a better chance."

The man acknowledged that perhaps he had worked his son too hard at times, which caused the boy to miss activities other youths enjoyed. He said his son loved sports, especially football, but his help was needed on the farm and he missed a lot of practice. Stacy dressed out for games but did not get to play much. Moreover, he had done well in track in North Carolina, but there was no track and field in Carroll County schools.

Ramsey said that in his son's senior year in high school, he had helped another man with his farm and that man "thought as much of him as I did." After high school, Stacy had worked for the man for a year until he found a construction job in Paris. He said his son was an "awful hard worker" who had never been in any trouble other than for two speeding tickets.

Father and son had incurred some problems as well, especially when Stacy had taken his truck off and wrecked it. Stacy had moved to Paris over that falling out, but came back home when his father broke a leg and needed help on the farm, though he kept the job in Paris. James Ramsey said his son helped out with bills and groceries while he was disabled with the broken leg.

Ramsey's stepmother, Sanna, said she came into his life when he was about nine. She said Stacy always did what was asked of him without question and had adjusted to her becoming his step-mom very easily, never giving her any trouble in thirteen years. As for her husband's disciplining of him, he had done that but not in an overly demanding way.

"He's my son, we love him," the woman sobbed. "If there was anything we could do to change it, we would."

Larry Ramer, a Paris plumbing contractor, told the jury that Ramsey had dated his daughter for three years. Ramsey was one of the most polite, respectful young men he had ever known and they had become buddies, Ramer said. Ramsey had spent the night at his house when there were large amounts of cash present, but that was never a concern.

"Do you think a lot of Stacy?" asked Maddox.

"I love him," Ramer replied.

John Ward, a neighbor of the Ramsey family, voiced similar words concerning the man's character.

"I think he's as fine a young man as I've ever known," Ward told the court. "If he could get out of here and go home today, he could move in with me . . . he was at the wrong place at the wrong time."

Ward said that at times, he had felt that "Mr. Ramsey might have been a little too hard on him." He had wished at times that his own sons were a little more well mannered like Stacy Ramsey.

Ward also believed Ramsey was easily influenced and maybe "a little slower than a lot of people. He had to think about things a little longer," Ward said.

Radford learned from Ward that he had been born in Alabama, and had moved to Carroll County from Illinois. He left Illinois because it was not a safe place to raise his children. As for Brooks' murder, it was "one of the worst things I ever heard of."

"It has changed Carroll County, hasn't it?" Radford inquired.

"Yes it has," Ward said, adding that he "probably had" told his sons not to stop to help people along the road now.

Eddie Bell, Ramsey's foreman at the Paris construction company where he worked, also had praise for Ramsey as a pleasant young man who did what he was told without complaint. He described him as very quiet and easy to get along with.

"I thought it couldn't be true when I heard he was arrested," said Bell. "I knew him too well."

Radford wondered what Ramsey did with the money he earned working. Bell said the boss was tight and did not pay top dollar. He did not know if Ramsey had been drinking a lot.

As for whether or not the crime had changed Bell's mind about helping people with car trouble along the road, the witness said that had changed over time with a number of occurrences, not just the latest crime.

Karen Jones, the wife of a Paris carpenter, told the court that Ramsey had lived with her family for several months beginning in December 1991, following the blowup with his father over the wrecked pickup. She described him as well-mannered, quiet and courteous at all times. He fell right in step with the house rules without even being told.

Maddox asked if Jones would describe Ramsey as a leader or a follower.

"I guess a follower," she answered. "Everybody liked him."

During closing arguments, Maddox implored the jury to give his client the straight life sentence.

"A life sentence slams the door, throws the key away for a minimum of twenty-five years," he said. "Don't throw him in the pot with Walter Smothers and Deion Harris. He's a better person than them."

Radford countered that the Brooks family deserved the mental security of knowing that the person responsible for their son's death was forever locked away.

"We cannot do that if you return a sentence of life," he said. "Either of the other two sentences can."

The jury deliberated two hours and twenty minutes before arriving at a sentence. Ramsey showed no emotion as he stood before Guinn and heard the pronouncement of life without the possibility of parole. He was ordered held by Carroll County until an opening could be found in the Department of

Corrections and was rushed from the courtroom by a bevy of Montgomery County deputies.

"We have suffered torment for the last ten months," Dennis Brooks said following the trial. "We will try to make the most of the time we have left."

Brooks said that his family did not consider the sentence vengeance, but an appropriate one made by the jury. He spoke of the great void the death of his son had created in the family's life.

We'll try to get up tomorrow and prepare ourselves for another day," he said. "Maybe it will heal someday."

With all three defendants found guilty and imprisoned, one might think the Dennis Brooks, Jr. murder case was at an end. However, such is not the case in the American judicial system. There are many, many avenues of appeal and most defendants take advantage of them to the fullest—even those who are as obviously guilty as the trio who brutally slaughtered young Brooks.

While the system is designed to make certain that the innocent are not inadvertently convicted and imprisoned (as they sometimes are, as proven by the many releases that have happened since DNA testing has been perfected) it is not unusual for the very guilty—or their attorneys—to drag things on for years.

That is not an indictment of lawyers or the legal profession. Indeed, the law requires them to afford their clients the very best defense they can mount and that precipitates the motions for new trials, appeals to higher courts and all the rest of it. Many attorneys on the losing end of a case can expect at some future point to find the defendant, with a new attorney at the helm, accusing the original lawyer of providing ineffective representation. No matter how good a job they attempt to do, no matter how sympathetic and kind they are to their clients, they become a deficit at some point. Of course, down the line, that would happen to the defense lawyers in the Brooks case.

The first step down the long road of appellate justice is the motion for a new trial. That rote action is filed in the same court where the defendant was convicted and before the same judge who has just presided over the case. And yes, you guessed it—it s very seldom successful. Nevertheless, it is one of the hoops that must be jumped through before proceeding further into the endless country of Appeal.

Thus, it was no surprise when West and Weems filed a motion for a new trial for Harris early in July. As certain as the outcome of a televised wrestling match, Judge Guinn denied it in no short order. West indicated the process would move on to the Court of Criminal Appeals in Jackson. The Maddox team filed a similar motion on Ramsey's behalf before Guinn a week later and met the exact same fate.

In a November ruling, the Court of Criminal Appeals unanimously upheld Harris' conviction, however, one judge expressed dissent on the life without parole sentence given Harris. Judge Gary R. Wade noted in a separate opinion that he could not go along with his colleagues on an issue concerning whether or not the jury found all parts of one of the aggravating circumstances applicable to reach that sentence.

That was one of thirteen issues raised by defense attorneys Weems and West, who questioned everything from improper indictment to improper comments made by DA Radford and Judge Guinn. Wade's variance came because of a circumstance requiring the crime to be "heinous, atrocious, or cruel in that it involved torture or serious abuse" before the death penalty or life without parole could be applied.

Wade noted that the circumstance was used to enhance Harris' punishment; however, he said that it was clear from the transcribed discussion between Judge Guinn and the jury foreman, upon return of the verdict, that not all the elements had been met. Guinn had said to the jury foreman that the entire aggravating circumstance had not been written out on the jury form; the jury had found that the murder was especially heinous and atrocious, but had omitted that it was cruel and involved serious physical abuse beyond that necessary to produce death.

"Is that what you intended it to be?" Guinn asked the foreman.

"Yes sir," the foreman responded.

"On the balance, I am unable to conclude beyond a reasonable doubt that the jury would have rendered the same sentence had they not considered the inappropriate aggravator, said Wade. "Accordingly, I would remand for resentencing. I do recognize that under these particular facts, the same sentence may very well occur."

Another enhancing factor had to do with whether or not the murder was committed to avoid detection and arrest. The court took note of the fact that Harris testified that Smothers said he shot the victim because he was afraid someone would hear the injured man and they would be caught. "The timing of the second shot supports the inference that it was done to avoid detection," the court found, also noting that the trio had managed to elude authorities in Hollow Rock after the murder.

Another bone of contention by the defense was that Judge Guinn had erred in not recusing himself because he had expressed partiality for a state witness, Agent Daniels, who had since died. The defense keyed in on comments Guinn had made about Daniels, such as "this man doesn't have a dishonest bone in his body" and "you couldn't beat a lie out of him" to support their contention that Guinn was prejudiced.

The appeals court saw some impropriety with Guinn's comments, though did not find that they rose to anything reversible.

"While this court does not condone the statements made by the experienced trial judge in this case, we are unable to find that it (sic) demonstrated a prejudice or bias which led to an unjust disposition of the case. We believe the comments were meant to be a tribute to a man in poor health whom the judge held in high regard . . . Although improper in a court setting, we find the appellant suffered no real prejudice as a result."

Radford's Jack London quote, "He who runs with the pack shares in the kill," also received some scrutiny, as the defense had taken exception to its use. The court ruled that while the quote likely gave the jury a "sharp visual image to relate to the alleged crime," it was particularly applicable in the context of felony murder.

"When viewed in light of the facts and circumstances, the statement was not inherently improper," the judges opined. "It was merely a description of the murder scene."

The appellant's questioning of improper argument by Radford during the sentencing phase of Harris' trial was less specific, maintaining only that the DA's argument was "a veiled proffer of vengeance." The court noted that while the Supreme Court had counseled against calls for vengeance by district attorneys ". . . in reading the district attorney's argument, we find no attempt to urge the jury to vengeance and the issue is without merit."

One issue raised was whether Guinn should have charged the jury with criminal facilitation, which could have been a lesser-included offense. The court found that argument without merit, noting that the appellant "was an active participant in the events leading up to the victim's murder and began the whole ordeal when she stopped Brooks in the road that night." The judges further noted that Harris kept a gun trained on Brooks at one point, and cursed and struck him as he lay on the roadway.

Another issue raised by the defense was the admission of post-death evidence—or what was done to the victim after his death. The argument was that Harris was not indicted for post-death acts, that the evidence was not necessary to prove murder, and that any value of the evidence was outweighed by the danger of prejudicing the jury.

While the court agreed that post-death facts were not necessary to prove the murder, those facts were relevant in proving Harris' role in the crime. The court noted that the facts showed she had opportunity to escape before the victim's body was desecrated, and that evidence found at her home made necessary the establishment of a chain of events that included the post-death acts.

"There is no question that the post-death evidence was gruesome and repulsive," the court agreed.

A contention by the defense that Guinn violated the Rules of Criminal Procedure during jury selection also went by the wayside, although the court found the judge in error and issued a note of caution. The error was that Guinn had seated twenty jurors in the box for the voir dire process, when the RCP limits the maximum number to twelve.

"Although the jury selection procedure employed was not in accordance with the Rules of Criminal Procedure, we find that the error was harmless . . . We caution the trial court and admonish against any future use of the procedure, but without a showing of prejudice, the error was harmless." The court added that the defense attorneys did not use all their allotted challenges during jury questioning in any case.

The defense's final issue centered on jurors being excluded for religious beliefs in opposition to capital punishment. The court found no error and cited a 1987 ruling by the Supreme Court addressing that issue.

In the case at hand, the appellate court ruled that the jurors were excused because their views on punishment did not allow them to follow the law as charged or to perform their duties as jurors bound by an oath, and not necessarily because of their religious views on the propriety of capital punishment.

There is no purpose found in belaboring the reader with more similar accounts of the many appeals that followed the one above, as all thus far have come to the same conclusion. The odds that any of the participants in Brooks' murder will ever gain release from custody so long as their bodies are still warm could be placed at somewhere between zero and never.

At one point, there did seem to be a brief glimmer of hope for Harris when she received a letter from Smothers in which he claimed he had lied about her involvement while on the witness stand. She got a post conviction relief hearing based on that, however, things went south in a hurry when Smothers told the court that he did not lie during his original testimony, but only claimed he had so that he could get out of prison for the day and take a ride.

And, in another development, Deion Harris managed to find herself another husband while behind bars. A retired airline pilot, Timothy McDonald, was traveling in Paris during one of her hearings and happened to go into the courthouse and catch part of it. He began to correspond with the woman and apparently, they fell in love and were later married in the prison chapel. Tennessee's prison system has no provision for conjugal visits, thus they are destined to forever have no contact more than a greeting hug and a bit of handholding during visits.

McDonald is convinced that his wife is innocent and has pledged to find a way to free her. He obviously has his work cut out for him. That diversion may replace conjugal enjoyment, but seems unlikely to bear fruit.

# AFTERWORD

Most of us have a mental "to do" list stashed away in some dark corner of our mind. Things we plan to do some day, although there is no timetable carved in stone. Very frequently, we never get around to completing those tasks and they go by the wayside. However, sometimes we do manage to address them. Writing a book about the Dennis Brooks, Jr. murder has been high on my list for many years.

I covered a number of murders during my 15 years as a reporter for *The McKenzie Banner*. All of them were shocking, because murder by its very nature is so alien—especially when it happens in a quiet rural area, where so little violence occurs.

Murders that happen in the heat of passion are easier to understand. A man catches his wife with another. Two men argue over a property line and tempers explode. Certainly, these are not good reasons to take a life but, in some primitive way, we can understand what led to them. People frequently act without thinking too much of the consequences. If they didn't, we wouldn't need so many courts, cops and lawyers.

Then, you have murders committed during the commission of some other crime, simply to eliminate witnesses. That's the hallmark of cold-blooded murder, the kind committed by psychopaths who have no conscience. Young Brooks had the misfortune to chance across a band of these individuals that fateful night, and yet that does not explain the full horror of his slaying.

No, the terrible desecration of his body afterward is what sets this murder apart. There was no reason for it, beyond satisfying the blood lust of at least one man who believed he had some connection to the forces of darkness and evil. A junior Lucifer wannabe.

The tendency in such cases is to blame the mayhem on drugs and alcohol. And, no doubt, they played a part; they helped free the monster lurking within. But, let's face it: if every drunken dope-head wandering around the countryside was capable of such despicable actions, it wouldn't be safe for any of us to leave our homes. Indeed, the rarity of such events proves the validity of that contention.

My objective in writing this book was not to construct some 500-page opus delving into the background and personality of everyone associated with the case. No, I simply wanted to construct a brief history of the case from the time of the victim's disappearance until the final trial concluded. And, I wanted to do so in the proper chronological order.

I relied on the twenty or so reporter notebooks I kept following the trials, along with the binder of newspaper galleys that I also maintained. More than 99-percent of the information related herein came from those sources. The bits about coroner Smith's past legal problems and Harris' jailhouse marriage I picked up from some television news broadcasts, which I'm sure many people saw and which I did not document at the time because, frankly, a book was still somewhere far down the road. I did obtain written permission from Mr. Rick Hollis, chair of the Dickson County Bicentennial Commission, to glean a brief bit of information from an article he wrote about Weems' esteemed relatives, and I thank him for that permission.

While I made no formal effort to interview anyone connected with the case, I did attempt to contact several people just to clarify a few points. My calls to one of the law officers involved went unreturned. That's not surprising. A producer of a television series doing a documentary on Harris told me she had to file court action against the county sheriff's department to obtain information. The authorities still consider the murder an open case because appeals continue to this day, some 16 years after the convictions. If that doesn't indicate the need for court reform, I don't have a clue what does.

One attorney I called refused to speak to me after I informed his receptionist about the nature of the call. I certainly couldn't blame him for not wanting to reopen that can of worms. Another did speak with me after I assured him I would not quote him, however, his memory of the events was so hazy that nothing was gained from the conversation.

Truth is, there is not much more to be learned about the bare facts of the case. There is no doubt that the proper people are in prison, where I suspect they will forever remain, appeals courts aside. The only question that hasn't been answered to my satisfaction is just when young Brooks was shot the first time. There were several different claims in that regard, all in conflict.

According to triggerman Smothers, the first shot was fired by accident as the truck was traveling down the highway shortly after the abduction, when he attempted to take the shotgun back from Harris. Ramsey accelerating suddenly was blamed in part for that. Of course, Smothers had earlier said that the shot happened after he slipped and fell.

Ramsey testified that he heard both gunshots before he even turned Brooks' pickup around. That would have meant the victim was dead before Keith and Jonnie Noles had their early morning encounter outside their home.

The Noles couple, who were not drunk and drugged, probably related the more accurate story of what transpired. They heard a shot and a scream while the vehicle was parked within one hundred feet or so from their house; that would have been the first shot, because Dennis Brooks, Jr. certainly could not have screamed after the second shot. The couple also saw the taillights as the truck departed north toward Hollow Rock after the gunfire and Investigator Bunn testified that he found blood splatters some twenty feet north on the roadway. Bunn also testified that he checked Ramsey's disabled truck four-tenths of a mile north of Noles' home, thus the couple certainly didn't see or hear anything that transpired at the original site of the abduction.

One interesting piece of testimony by Keith Noles was how he heard a male voice say, "If you move this truck I'll blow your goddamn head off." Since Smothers admittedly had control of the shotgun from the beginning, logic would dictate it was he who uttered that comment. And, since the pickup was near Noles' house and pointing north, logic would also dictate that Smothers was yelling at Ramsey, not Brooks.

That possibility was never addressed. Maybe Ramsey had good reason to fear Smothers. We will likely never know for sure.

May 3, 2010
Jim Chandler
McKenzie, Tennessee

Jim Chandler is a retired newspaper reporter and a native of McKenzie, Tennessee. His poems and stories have appeared in numerous small and literary magazines and anthologies in America and abroad. He is the author of the poetry collection *Smoke & Thunder* and a novel, *Parallel Blues*, as well as several chapbooks. In 2006, he undertook a 2,300-mile road trip to video tape poets in North Carolina, Pennsylvania, Michigan and Ohio and spent a year editing it into a two-hour documentary, "Poetry Road -- In Search of the Word." He is currently revising another novel.

Made in the USA
Coppell, TX
08 May 2022

77572585R00069